HEINEMANN

Britain

51

Edited by

Peter Catterall

Heinemann

HISTO... ...EFINGS

Heinemann Educational
a division of Heinemann Publishers (Oxford) Ltd.
Halley Court, Jordan Hill, Oxford OX2 8EJ

OXFORD LONDON EDINBURGH
MELBOURNE MADRID ATHENS
BOLOGNA PARIS SYDNEY
AUCKLAND SINGAPORE TOKYO
IBADAN NAIROBI HARARE
GABORONE PORTSMOUTH NH (USA)

First published 1994

British Library Cataloguing in Publication Data

A catalogue record for this book is available from the British Library

ISBN 0 435 31002 X

98 97 96 95 94
10 9 8 7 6 5 4 3 2 1

Typeset by CentraCet Ltd, Cambridge

Printed in Great Britain by Clay Ltd, St Ives plc.

Front cover: *The General Strike* by Cliff Rowe (reproduced by kind permission of Paul Gallagher, General Secretary of the A.E.E.U.).

Acknowledgements

Heinemann and the ICBH wish to thank all the contributors who have given permission for their work to be published in this book.

Thanks are also due to Philip Allan (Publishers) Ltd for permission to print articles which originally appeared in the *Modern History Review*.

Contents

Introduction

Most villages, and many of the churches, chapels, schools and workplaces of Britain contain a memorial to the dead of the First World War. Some 745,000 British servicemen were killed in this war. Many others were damaged in body or mind. Despite the introduction of the new science of psychology in the late nineteenth century, however, appreciation of the problems of the mind was still in its infancy. The condition of shell-shock, post-traumatic stress, was only slowly diagnosed during the war. Whilst therapies to treat the scarring of the mind were gradually developed it was not until the Second World War that the development of plastic surgery enabled attempts to remedy the more ghastly scarrings of the body. Of those who survived the First World War, all too many never recovered.

Not since the Napoleonic Wars had Britain made a comaprable military commitment to the maintenance of the balance of power in Europe. The First World War saw the largest armies Britain had ever mustered, with conscription introduced for the first time in 1916. An unprecedented continental commitment continued into peacetime, with the last British occupying troops in the Rhineland not leaving until 1930.

The Home Front did not escape the war's effects. Early in the war, before the growth of British aircraft production, Zeppelins raided as far north as Bradford. The war initially exposed deficiencies in the production of aircraft, chemicals, motor vehicles and other forms of material and then acted as a catalayst for the development of these industries. At the same time it led to unprecedented mobilisation for war production. Fears that economic dislocation would lead to unemployment proved unfounded; instead men in some skilled crafts had to be brought back from the front. The need to maintain production led to closer government relations with the trade unions and encouraged some employers, for the first time, to recognise and negotiate with these bodies. Trade unionism grew dramatically in numbers and prestige. Labour relations, however, were complicated by high wartime inflation, which also hit some professional groups. In particular, there was resentment at inflated profits for business, whilst the working classes suffered from the consequence of higher prices. This reinforced Left-wing demands for greater state control of private industry.

The need to ensure production, meanwhile, led to the extension of State control into new areas. Ministries sprang up to organise food, munitions, shipping or labour and to promote scientific and industrial research. The overhaul of the machinery of the State extended right to the top. In December 1916, the incoming Lloyd George coalition introduced the Cabinet Office for the central co-ordination of goverment. The Forestry Commission was created and coal mines and railways were taken into government control. A complex propaganda machine was gradually developed, starting in 1914 with efforts particularly directed at ensuring the sympathy of the USA and, if possible, American participation on the Allied side.

Although a number of these administrative innovations survived 1918, the propaganda machinery was rapidly dismantled at the end of the war. There was also a return, albeit less complete, to pre-war norms in the field of economic policy. Protection, supported by the new manufacturing interests which thrived under the McKenna Duties introduced in 1915, such as the motor industry, was defeated at the 1923 election and dismantled by the ensuing Labour government. It was not until after Britain had been forced off the Gold Standard in 1931 that it finally ousted free trade. Taxation was reduced, and though it continued at a higher level than before the war the major beneficiary was social expenditure, whilst defence spending was pared, with significant consequences in the 1930s. Even the expansion of social expenditure was constrained. In 1918, Fisher's Education Act raised the school leaving age for all children to fourteen, and envisaged a school leaving age of fifteen and continuation schools to eighteen. This was followed by the 1919 Housing Act of Christopher Addison, the wartime Minister of Reconstruction, which introduced Treasury subsidies for housing provision by local authorities. Both of these measures were, however, to be emasculated during the economic crisis which, in 1920–21, quickly succeeded a short-lived post-war boom.

The boom of 1919–20 was accentuated by the desire to catch up on wartime inflation and the relaxation of wartime controls. The result was a series of bitter labour disputes capped, in August 1920, by the formation of the Communist Party. A worried government was prompted to deploy troops and, in 1920, introduce the Emergency Powers Act. Meanwhile, the boom stoked up more inflation, leading the government to raise interest rates to choke off demand. The 'Geddes Axe' was also introduced to reduce government expenditure. This exacerbated the succeeding downturn. By 1921 returned soldiers were marching in demonstrations of the unemployed with the numbers on the Poor Law peaking at 1.7 million that autumn. The coal industry found itself in difficulty mainly because reparations coal from Germany hit British exports. The

Miners' Federation's solution of nationalisation of an under-capitalised and fragmented industry, narrowly supported by the Sankey Royal Commission in 1919, was rejected by the Lloyd George government. The only solution the coalowners could see was to reduce the miners' wages – an attack on working class living standards which led to the General Strike in 1926.

The subsequent defeat of the General Strike and the miners brought to an end the period of industrial militancy which had begun before the First World War. The resulting distress in the coalfields, however, compounded the effects of that other bane of the inter-war years, unemployment. Unemployment in the 1920s became for the first time a significant election issue, though diminishing in electoral importance in the 1930s, possibly because of the failure of the 1929–31 Labour government to tackle it. It had already become a more significant policy issue. As early as 1915 a temporary out of work donation was devised to ease the process of demobilisation at the end of the war. This was extended, in 1920, into a scheme of unemployment insurance covering all workers except agricultural labourers, domestic servants and the Civil Service. The sustained high and unanticipated levels of unemployment that appeared from that year, however, meant that the insurance principle had constantly to be supplemented by doles and transitional benefits. The cost of this was a major factor in the budget crisis that brought down the Labour government in 1931.

Falling food prices did, however, help to ease the poverty and distress caused by unemployment. For those in employment, resulting higher disposable incomes could be spent on new consumer goods (there were 2 million cars and 11 million wireless licences by 1939) and leisure activities, such as the cinema or the football pools. This trend was encouraged in the 1930s by low interest rates and the introduction of new forms of consumer credit. Cheap mortgages and cheap materials produced a building boom. In all some four million houses were built between the wars, the majority in the 1930s.

Despite the relative cheapness of houses in the 1930s and the explicit link, after 1930, of subsidised building with slum clearance, new houses were still often too expensive for all but the better-off working class. At the same time many houses, in rural as well as urban areas, remained inadequate. The housing problem was to be exacerbated during the Second World War, not least because of the effects of bombing. Half a million houses were destroyed and over three million damaged. Opinion polls, introduced from America in 1937, made it clear that housing was far the most important issue in the 1945 election.

Reconstruction in the wake of the destruction of the war years was even more of a necessity after this second great conflict. The incoming Labour government took the opportunity to decant population from over-crowded and bomb-damaged London to a ring of new towns. Industrial development was directed towards the areas which had suffered high unemployment in the 1930s in a far more thoroughgoing way than the first tentative steps in regional policy by the National government from 1934 onwards. These policies reflected governmental efforts to produce industrial as well as social reconstruction. Planning controls and nationalisation were, from the 1930s, increasingly being argued for on the Left on grounds of efficiency, rather than social justice. The resulting nationalisations of infrastructure industries such coal, transport, water and the Bank of England took place against a world economic background which was much less severe than that experienced in 1918–22. American investment, in contrast to American insistence on repayment of war debts after the First World War, ensured steady expansion. The British economy was, however, constrained by the need to export to earn dollars to repay US loans and buy American products. The resulting austerity compounded dissatisifaction with shortcomings in the housing programme. These shortcomings were fully exploited by Conservative propaganda. The Conservative revival saw party membership and partisanship for both major parties at heights not seen since. It culminated when, despite winning slightly fewer votes than Labour, the Conservatives squeezed to victory in October 1951 on their slogan, *Set the People free*.

Part I
Political Realignment

At the outbreak of the First World War the Liberals were still firmly in control of government, despite a minority in Parliament. The Conservatives were frustrated by years of opposition and the Labour party was still a ginger group, making progress in some local elections but unable to put up sufficient candidates really to challenge in the parliamentary arena. The first casualty of the war was the unity of the Labour Party. An ILP faction led by MacDonald argued that Britain should have remained neutral. MacDonald shared with various Liberals, such as E.D. Morel, the view that Britain had drifted into war because of secret diplomatic undertakings. The resulting formation of the Union of Democratic Control in 1914 became a route by which a number of Liberals eventually joined Labour.

Generally, however, Liberal unity was maintained for the first year of the war and, when Asquith was obliged to broaden the administration in May 1915, the Liberals remained in control of the bulk of the portfolios. More damaging was the crisis of December 1916, which saw Asquith replaced as Prime Minister, though not as leader of the Liberal Party, by Lloyd George. Asquith subsequently gave little leadership to his followers. Liberal newspapers like *The National* complained in August 1918 that the Liberal frontbench acted, 'intermittently or not at all'. This Liberal weakness created the opportunity for Labour to break out of the electoral strait jacket it had been in before the war.

Political parties were already being faced by the need to reorganise. The decay of the electoral registers during the wartime political truce led to the invention of a new constitutional device, an all-party Speaker's Conference, to address the problem. This agreed to introduce universal franchise for males over 21, to give the parliamentary vote to women over 30 with property qualifications under the pre-war franchise (extended to all women over 21 in 1928) and to redistribute many seats. This arrangement reflected horse-trading between the parties over the likely benefits. It used to be thought that Labour were the major beneficiaries of the resulting 1918 Representation of the People Act. The pre-war electorate, however, was overwhelmingly working class, and the new legislation made it only marginally more so. It was not the new voters so much as the redistribution of seats that was important; the sub-division of suburban constituencies creating a solid base for the inter-war Conservative Party. The Conservatives further benefited in 1921 from the excision of Ireland from the United Kingdom, thereby removing a block of opponents from the Commons.

The wartime redistribution also prompted reorganisation in the Labour Party. Constituency parties were formed and, encouraged by the Liberal disarray, there was a dramatic increase in Labour candidates. Liberal morale and finances were weak, and the grass-roots of the Party were sapped by local anti-Labour alliances with the Tories. Traditional issues such as Home Rule or Welsh disestablishment were resolved. Even free trade, which re-united the Liberals in 1923, very rapidly disappeared as an issue after it was replaced by imperial preference in 1932. Instead, new issues such as unemployment and industrial conflict emerged. In these circumstances a large number of Liberals turned to the Conservatives, reassured by Stanley Baldwin's language of social peace and unity in the face of class conflict at home and the appearance of the Soviet Union abroad. In the process the Liberal-led Progressive Alliance of the Edwardian period was replaced by a Tory-led anti-Labour alliance, which proved to be even more successful.

Kenneth O. Morgan

British Politics and War

The First World War transformed the British political landscape, threw up new leaders and destroyed the political careers of others. British politics and political culture would never be the same again.

The Great War as it later came to be known, marked an immense watershed in British politics. Yet at first it seemed almost to abolish political activity altogether. At the time of Britain's entry into the war in August 1914, the two main parties were ferociously at odds, over labour unrest, the Welsh Church, but most of all Home Rule for Ireland, where the Unionists of Protestant Ulster and the Catholics in the rest of the island seemed on the brink of civil war. The Liberal government under Asquith (with 261 MPs), backed up by the Irish Nationalists (with 84) and Labour (with 37) seemed locked in intense conflict with the Unionists or Conservatives (with their 287 MPs) in a way not seen since the 1832 Reform Act.

Then, on 4 August, the dramatic announcement of Britain's declaration of war on Germany and Austria-Hungary transformed the situation. Political partisanship was suspended forthwith, the war itself became immensely popular for some time, and antiwar dissenters like the Labour leaders, Keir Hardie and Ramsay MacDonald, were denounced as traitors. The Liberal government suspended its two highly controversial measures, the disestablishment of the Welsh Church and Home Rule for Ireland, while local party organisation went into abeyance. A strange, unreal lull in politics resulted. The most radical member of Asquith's cabinet, David Lloyd George, the Chancellor of the Exchequer, who had strongly condemned the war in South Africa fourteen years earlier, now vehemently backed the war effort. Indeed, he claimed it to be a struggle for liberal values, and the rights of 'little five foot five nations' such as Belgium, Serbia and Montenegro, a battle for civilisation itself.

But the pause in political life could not last. In particular, the fact that the war went so badly from the outset focused criticism on the government's war strategy and on the leadership of Asquith himself. He had been an imposing peacetime Premier, but seemed lethargic during the crisis of war. The effect of normal party activity being suspended resulted in debate and partisan comment being focused on the newspapers instead. The *Daily Chronicle*, *Morning Post* and especially Lord Northcliffe's *The Times* became vehicles for leaks, rumours and innuendo. Following the disastrous dispatch of an Allied expedition to the Dardanelles (with which Winston Churchill, the First Lord of the Admiralty, was strongly linked), a crisis blew up in May 1915.

The ostensible cause lay in a furious dispute between Churchill and Lord Fisher, the imperious First Sea Lord. Behind it, though, lay a long record of discontent and unease within the government and on the backbenches. In particular, there was much anxiety over the munitions supply and 'shell shortage' on the western front. In a complex episode on 17–19 May 1915, the Unionist leader, Bonar Law, put pressure on Asquith to remodel his government on a coalition basis. Asquith responded in his own terms by strengthening the Liberals' position, by making Reginald McKenna Chancellor of the Exchequer, while the key figure of Lloyd George, in a crucial phase, agreed to move to a new Ministry of Munitions. Unionists now entered the government and so, for the first time, did Labour. But the fragile period of non-partisan 'unity' had been shattered. British wartime politics were henceforth a prey to intrigue and long-term instability, with profound and enduring consequences.

From Asquith to Lloyd George 1915–16

The making of the coalition had seemed at first to place Asquith in a stronger position. But ultimately it proved fatal for him. Strains were placed on the morale of the Liberal Party. Divisions opened up between government ministers and backbenchers with their journalistic and (sometimes) military allies. Above all, new tensions developed between Lloyd George and Asquith, the former increasingly finding his closest associates among non-party press lords and businessmen, and indeed within the ranks of the Unionists.

The issue that, above all others, promoted party conflict was that of military conscription. To all Unionists and, to an increasing degree, to Lloyd George and a group of Liberal pro-war supporters, national service appeared the ultimate symbol of the rigorous all-out prosecution of the war, of a 'knock-out blow' and a 'fight to a finish'. Throughout the autumn and winter of 1915–16, argument raged within the administration; the gulf between Asquith and Lloyd George widened all the time. In January 1916, Asquith had to surrender the major concession of proposing military conscription for single men only; even this cost the government a leading Liberal minister, Sir John Simon, the Home Secretary. Dispute went on, however, and in April Asquith had to concede the general principle of conscription for all males between the ages of 18 and 45, other than certain exempted categories. But the entire affair made him appear indecisive, and relations with Lloyd George ever more frigid.

Indeed, an unofficial list of parliamentary Liberals prepared to endorse the Welshman as Premier was drawn up at this time.

The war still went very badly. The British army suffered catastrophic losses on the Somme; the expedition in Salonika was another huge failure; Kitchener, the Secretary for War, was drowned in the North Sea, and Lloyd George took his place, clearly the coming man, in the government. In the autumn, the overrunning of Rumania by German and Austrian forces seemed a further sign of faltering British leadership. Meanwhile the course of events in Ireland, where the suppression of the Easter Rising in Dublin gave a stimulus to an extreme republican movement, Sinn Fein, added more fuel to criticisms of Asquith's style of Premiership.

Then, between 1 and 9 December 1916, Asquith was overthrown as Prime Minister in favour of Lloyd George. The crisis originated with an attempt by Lloyd George and two leading Unionists, Bonar Law and the Ulster leader, Sir Edward Carson, to remodel the government by creating a supreme war council to run the war. At first Asquith seemed to agree, but then went back on the idea, since it appeared to tie his hands; a trial of strength now took place. In the event, Lloyd George won the endorsement not only of almost all the Unionists, but also, critically, of about half the Liberal MPs, shrewdly marshalled by Dr Christopher Addison, one of Lloyd George's closest associates. Crucially too, on 9 December, the Labour Party, whose role had become stronger with the new importance of the trade unions in the war economy, also narrowly agreed to join the government. A five-man war cabinet was now created, with Lloyd George, the three Unionists, Bonar Law, Lord Curzon and Lord Milner, and the Labour leader, Arthur Henderson as its members. A new centralised structure of wartime command was created. It left the Liberal Party, which had governed since 1905, divided and demoralised. British politics since December 1916 have never been the same again.

Lloyd George's wartime ascendancy

At the outset, Lloyd George's position was most precarious. He was a Prime Minister without a party, dependent on the Unionists, with Asquith on the opposition benches, and dangerous freebooters like Churchill on the flanks. His priority was survival. For 18 months, his authority seemed most uncertain. But he had one great asset – the widespread view that, in spite of continuing military defeats in France, he alone was 'the man who could win the war'. From that time onwards his political ascendancy was the motor of change and the dominant fact of British public life for some years to come.

The new Prime Minister was a remote quasi-presidential figure, surrounded by a kind of Welsh Mafia in Downing Street. His position was underpinned by two institutional novelties – a newly-formed cabinet secretariat headed by Sir Maurice Hankey, and a Prime Minister's secretariat, the so-called 'garden suburb' (or kitchen cabinet in the language of a later generation), private advisers who worked intimately with him in No. 10. Apart from the war cabinet of five, he also brought in an array of industrialists and businessmen like Sir Eric Geddes, Lord Rhondda and Lord Devonport to run government departments, while he even called in General Jan Smuts from South Africa as a cabinet member to underline the imperial dimension of wartime government. Meanwhile party politics continued to be prey to intrigue and rumour, in Parliament and even more in the press. Prolonged dispute between Lloyd George and his main generals, Haig and Robertson, added to the uncertainties of his government. Churchill was able to re-enter the government in July 1917, but, damagingly, Labour's Arthur Henderson left it in August, following a dispute with Lloyd George over relations with the new post-revolution government in Russia. It was an episode of long-term significance.

Until the summer of 1918 it was totally unclear what kind of politics would emerge after the war was over. In the constituencies, political machinery was falling into disarray, especially among the divided Liberals. Then a turning-point came in May 1918. After General Maurice had accused the government in the newspapers of withholding reserves from the British Army in France, a fateful division took place in the Commons during the Ludendorff offensive that spring. Lloyd George routed his opponents with a slashing speech, but 98 Liberals voted against the government and a new divide in politics opened up. Two months later, the government's Liberal chief whip, Captain Freddie Guest, negotiated a secret electoral pact with the Unionists to form the basis of a coalition arrangement at the next general election, under which 'Coalition Liberal' supporters of Lloyd George would have a free run in up to 150 seats without Unionist opposition; this was derisively referred to as 'the coupon' of coalition approval.

As the fortunes of war turned, following the entry of the Americans and the final push to victory by Haig and Marshal Foch in the autumn of 1918, it became clear that post-war politics would now have to be defined anew. Between 7 and 9 November, just before the armistice, Lloyd George's Liberal ministers were persuaded to agree to fight the next election in coalition with the Unionists on a joint platform. This duly took place in the so-called 'coupon election' of December. It was a strangely unreal contest, marred by some jingoistic hysteria against the defeated enemy with calls for 'hanging the Kaiser' and 'squeezing Germany till the pips squeaked'. In opposition to the government were the 'pacifists' and the 'Bolsheviks' so-called, a minority rump of Asquithian Liberals and the Labour Party which, fatefully for them, had decided to leave Lloyd George's government at the end of the war, following Bernard Shaw's famous appeal: 'Go back to Lloyd George and say nothing doing.' The election was fought on a hugely expanded electorate of 21 million, with 8 million women over thirty receiving the vote for the first time. The result was a landslide, with over 520 supporters of the coalition returned, as against only 63 Labour and 28 Independent Liberals. In Ireland, Sinn Fein swept the board, returning 73 MPs who refused to attend Westminster. Lloyd George seemed utterly dominant. Bonar Law commented at this time: 'He can be Prime Minister for life if he likes.'

Lloyd George's peacetime ascendancy 1919–20

For the moment, Lloyd George seemed the unique arbiter of British politics. He remained detached from Westminster and Whitehall, surrounded by advisers and cronies in the garden suburb and elsewhere. Until the end of July, he was mostly away at the Paris Peace Conference which resulted in the controversial Treaty of Versailles. His government operated against a background of much uncertainty with virtual war breaking out in Ireland between the British forces and their auxiliaries, and the Irish Republican Army which backed Sinn Fein. There was also violent confrontation at home between trade unions and employers in the mines, railways and elsewhere. The Liberal opposition under Asquith (who had lost his seat but was returned at a by-election for Paisley in 1920) remained shattered by its wartime traumas; the Unionists had many rumblings of discontent on its right wing, not yet serious. The one clearly growing force was the Labour Party, which began to displace the Liberals in industrial constituencies in several by-elections. But, in a mood of 'national government' fostered by the Olympian Prime Minister, it seemed that pre-war partisan politics were a thing of the past. The emphasis was now on an international settlement and 'reconstruction' at home to build that 'land fit for heroes' of which Lloyd George had spoken at the election.

But the contours of the political landscape remained unclear. The coalition was, in fact, inherently unstable. Relations in the government between Liberal and Unionist ministers were strained. In the Commons, they were even more so. Liberal and Unionist whips maintained separate machinery, eyeing each other warily. One factor that would bring them together, notoriously, was money, since both indulged in the sale of honours to rich (sometimes criminal) capitalists, to build up their party funds. This was particularly essential for Lloyd George if he was to have any future in Politics.

In early 1920 the Premier tried to create a more permanent base. Using the wartime analogy of 'unity of command' he urged that the logic of a national government was a national party. He therefore urged the 'fusion' of the two wings of the coalition. Bonar Law and the Unionists, themselves also shattered by the experience of war, seemed disposed to agree. However, quite unexpectedly, the Liberal ministers turned the idea down, preferring to retain their old commitment to social reform and especially to free trade. The outcome, however, was renewed division between Coalitionist and Asquithian Liberals which continued to rage for years to come and which focused on the ever controversial character of the Prime Minister, including his party 'fund'. He himself continued to use the rhetoric of coalition, and when Bonar Law was replaced by Austen Chamberlain as Unionist leader in March 1921 (Bonar Law's ill-health had apparently led to his permanent withdrawal from front-line politics), the move for realignment gained some momentum. But British politics remained in flux. The transition from wartime to peacetime had yet to be made.

Downfall of the coalition 1921–22

The next two years saw the coalition buffeted by rival pressures, and the rapid resumption of party politics after six years of deceptive 'unity'. The government's policies seemed to fall into disarray. At home, the economy deteriorated and mass unemployment resulted. The trade unions remained sullen and hostile, especially after the collapse of a move for the general strike on 'Black Friday' (15 April 1921). Ireland remained a hopeless *impasse*, torn apart by violence and political conflict. Overseas, Lloyd George's desperate efforts to restore the comity of nations, including the development of commerical relations with Soviet Russia, seemed unavailing.

The coalition was now assailed from left and right. Labour was joined by progressive Liberals in denouncing the government for the betrayal of its social pledges and the 'Geddes Axe' of economies which made severe inroads into social spending. The policy of repression in Ireland also seemed to confirm that Lloyd George could no longer project himself as a man of the left. On the right, he was assailed with even more ferocity. Whereas the left attacked him for making war in Ireland, many unionists turned against the government for reversing policy and concluding peace terms in December 1921 with the representatives of Sinn Fein. From January 1922, the 26 counties of southern Ireland becmae an independent Free State, which many Unionists saw as a betrayal of all they stood for in public life. 'Anti-Waste' Tories attacked Liberal ministers for extravagant expenditure. Meanwhile, the attempt to restore diplomatic relations with Russia at the Genoa Conference also aroused passionate right-wing opposition.

The Prime Minister's style caused even more resentment than his policies. His political unorthodoxy (on one occasion the British cabinet met in Inverness town hall), his air of contempt for the conventions of public life, his association with press lords, all raised concern. His unconventionality was underlined by the honours system, in which the Prime Minister's aides openly sold titles and peerages in return for contributions to party funds. Many felt this to be in defiance of the royal prerogative in creating peers. In the summer of 1922, with right-wing opposition to the Premier's adventurisms reaching a crescendo, Lloyd George's future seemed in jeopardy.

What the right-wing rebels needed was a credible leader. In October, they found one. The final source of crisis came when Lloyd George took Britain almost to the brink of war with Turkey in promoting his obsession with the Greek cause in Asia Minor. A series of Unionist ministers indicated their concern, headed by the Foreign Secretary, Lord Curzon, whom Lloyd George had frequently humiliated. Out of the shadows came the old leader, Bonar Law, whose letter to *The Times* on 7 October 1922 warned that Britain could not alone act as 'policeman of the world'. A meeting called by the Unionist leader, Austen Chamberlain, at the Carlton Club on 19 October, backfired badly. A little-known minister, Stanley Baldwin, condemned the Prime Minister as 'a dynamic force' which, declared Baldwin, was 'a very terrible thing'. The Unionist MP's voted by 185 to 88 to break with the coalition. Lloyd George resigned the same day. Though few recognised it at the time, it was the end of an era of personal government.

Conclusion

The ensuing general election saw the Conservatives return to office with Bonar Law as Prime Minister. They held 344 seats, while Labour emerged as the clear opposition, rising to 142. The Liberals were deeply divided between the rival supporters of Asquith and Lloyd George, with the former gaining 62 seats and the lattter 53. Liberal candidates lost heavily to Labour in industrial regions of the North, Scotland and South Wales. The age of coalition was over; partisanship returned.

Even so, the impact of war transformed the nature of party politics. The Conservatives and Labour were now the main contenders for power, headed respectively by Stanley Baldwin and

Ramsay MacDonald. These two had in common the fact that each of them represented an ideological reaction to Lloyd George and all his words. Conversely, the Liberals emerged from the deluge having suffered fundamental damage from which they have never really recovered. The divisions between Asquithians and Lloyd Georgians continued to fester, despite a shot-gun reunion in December 1923; arguments on such matters as the 'Lloyd George fund' continued to divide them. Beyond Westminster, Liberal organisation went into decay. Many of their businessmen supporters now found it prudent to endorse the Conservatives, since the conflict between capital and labour had transcended older issues like free trade, temperance or religious questions. In social terms, many of the sources of pre-war Liberalism were in rapid decline – the nonconformist chapels, the Celtic nationalism of Scotland and Wales, West-country rural radicalism, above all the staple industries of mining, textiles and shipbuilding. The Liberals were henceforth no longer a party of government. They were a major casualty of total war.

Another important change was that Ireland no longer overshadowed British politics. The creation of the Irish Free State naturally ended southern Irish representation in Westminster and thereby a crucial balancing factor in British politics. In practice, this meant that many Catholic voters in such areas as Lancashire or Clydeside turned to Labour, class replacing religion or ethnicity as the focus of allegiance. Only in 1968 did the Ulster problem re-emerge.

Perhaps the most striking impact of all was the change of mood that the war brought about. In the new mass politics, heralded by the expansion of the electorate and votes for women, a more critical attitude emerged. It was first directed at Lloyd George and his generals, but in time Baldwin and MacDonald, the apparent victors of 1922, suffered a similar slump in their reputations. Even Churchill, the hero of the Second World War was, until 1938, popularly distrusted as the architect of the Dardanelles fiasco. British post-war politics implied a somewhat disenchanted universe. From that time onwards, it would never be glad confident morning again, as the British people faced up to a scenario of late imperial decline.

Further Reading

Blake, R. *The Conservative Party from Peel to Thatcher* (Fontanta Press, 1985).
Morgan, K.O. *The Age of Lloyd George* (Allen and Unwin, 1978).
Morgan, K.O. *Consensus and Disunity: the Lloyd George Coalition Government, 1918–22* (Oxford University Press, 1986).

Pugh, M. *The Making of Modern British Politics*, 1867–1939 (Blackwell, 1982).
Ramsden, J. *The Age of Balfour and Baldwin, 1902–40* (Longman, 1978).
Tanner, D. *Political Change and the Labour Party, 1900–18* (Cambridge University Press, 1990).
Turner, J. *British Politics and the Crisis of War* (Yale University Press, 1992).
Wrigley, C. *Lloyd George and the Challenge of Labour: the Post-war Coalition, 1918–22* (Harvester Press, 1992).

Kenneth O. Morgan is Vice-Chancellor of the University of Wales.

Paul Adelman

The Decline of the Liberal Party 1910–31

Historians have long debated the causes of the political realignment which engulfed the Liberal Party after 1914. But why did it happen, and when did the Liberals pass the point of no return?

After the great landslide victory of 1906, 400 Liberal MPs were returned to the House of Commons. But four years later in the general election of December 1910, the Liberals were reduced to 272 MPs, the same total as the Conservatives, and were only able to continue as the governing party with the support of Labour and the Irish. Owing to the split between the supporters of Asquith and those of Lloyd George in the elections of 1918 and 1922, it is difficult to assess the real strength of Liberalism in the immediate post-war years, though on the most favourable interpretation of the figures it appears that the Liberals were now in third place behind Labour.

A fairer verdict is available in the general election of 1923. Then, the two sections of the Liberal Party reunited under the leadership of Asquith in the defence of free trade, and experienced a real revival, winning 159 seats and about 30% of the popular vote – only a hair's breadth behind Labour! Nevertheless, owing to the first-past-the-post system, Labour gained 191 seats and the Conservatives 258, leaving the Liberals still in last place. The general election of 1924 drove home the message of decline: the Liberals were decimated and reduced to 40 MPs. Even the brilliant campaign conducted by Lloyd George in 1929 (following the death of Asquith in the previous year) could not give the Liberals more than 59 seats, even though there were more than 500 candidates standing – almost as many as in the miracle year of 1906. Thereafter, Liberal decline seemed inexorable: 21 MPs in 1935, 12 in 1945

The Strange Death of Liberal England

It has been argued by some writers, notably George Dangerfield in his melodramatic *Strange Death of Liberal England* (1935), that the seeds of Liberal decline were already apparent in the years 1910–14. They argue that the Liberal Party was faced with a combination of problems – opposition of the House of Lords, labour unrest, suffragette militancy, armed opposition in Ireland – which, together, fatally undermined its strength and confidence.

Parties	1918[1]	1922[2]	1923	1924	1929	1931[3]	1935[4]	1945
Lib Vote	2,754,448	4,189,527	4,311,147	2,928,747	5,308,510	2,318,510	1,422,116	2,248,226
% share	25.6	29.1	29.6	17.6	23.4	10.7	6.4	9.0
Cands	411	490	453	340	513	160	161	306
MPs	161	116	159	40	59	72	21	12
Lab Vote	2,385,472	4,241,383	4,438,508	5,489,077	8,389,512	6,649,630	8,325,491	11,995,152
% share	22.2	29.5	30.5	33.0	37.1	30.6	37.9	47.8
Cands	388	411	422	512	571	515	552	604
MPS	63	142	191	151	288	52	154	393
Con Vote	3,874,573	5,500,382	5,538,824	8,039,598	8,656,473	11,978,745	11,810,158	9,988,306
% share	36.0	38.2	38.1	48.3	38.2	55.2	53.7	39.8
Cands	411	483	540	552	590	523	585	624
MPs	350	345	258	419	260	473	432	213

General Election Statistics 1915–45

Notes:

1. Liberal figures are for both Asquithians and Lloyd Georgians. There were 133 Lloyd Georgians and 28 Asquithians.
2. Liberal figures are for both Asquithians and Lloyd Georgians. There were 62 Lloyd Georgians and 54 Asquithians, though the latter comfortably outpolled the Lloyd Georgians, encouraging the re-merger in 1923.
3. Liberal figures include Liberal Nationals (Simonites) Liberals (Samuelites) and a small independent group consisting of Lloyd George and his family.
4. Conservative figures for both 1935 and 1945 include those for National Liberals (as the Simonites had become after 1931).

Source: David Butler and Gareth Butler, *British Political Facts 1900–1985*, (Macmillan, 1986).

Today, this argument seems hopelessly exaggerated. The Liberal government coped tolerably well with the problems that faced it on the domestic front, and it can hardly be blamed for not 'solving' the Irish problem. Nor is there any hard evidence for the supposed demoralisation of the Liberal Party. Asquith's leadership was unquestioned; his government remained strong, unified and confident – not one minister resigned before the outbreak of war; and its radical policies continued, as Lloyd George's Land Campaign and 1914 Budget show.

Nor were the future electoral prospects of the Liberal Party as damning as the statistics might suggest. It is true that the party lost more than 100 seats in the 1910 elections and another 15 to the Tories in by-elections over the next four years. But many of these were middle-class seats which (like Labour in 1945) the Liberals had only won in 1906 due to general disillusionment with the Conservative record.

What is more relevant is that the Liberal Party was able to build up support among the working class during the whole Edwardian period, and this was largely due to the impact of the 'New Liberalism' with its programme of state-sponsored social reform. The Liberals' successful appeal at this level meant that the new Labour Party found it extraordinarily difficult to challenge its dominance in working-class seats outside the 30 or so constituencies where it had been given a free run by the Liberals in 1906 under the terms of the Lib-Lab Pact of 1903. Labour was indeed hard pressed to win any seats against Liberal candidates at the general elections of 1910; it came bottom of the poll and lost three seats to the Liberals at the 12 by-elections it fought over the next four years. The Liberal Party may have been losing ground to the right, but it was warding off the challenge from the left. It would therefore be false to conclude that we are faced with a Liberal Party in decline in the years preceding the First World War. Nor was it entirely fanciful for one Liberal MP to assert: 'The present government has beaten the record of all modern governments by winning three general elections. We believe that we shall win the fourth when it comes along.'

A rampant omnibus

If, then, the Liberal Party was in reasonably good shape in 1914, it is tempting to argue that it was the First World War itself that was the agent of Liberal decline – the 'rampant omnibus' (in Professor Trevor Wilson's famous metaphor) that knocked down and ran over the Liberal Party. 'The outbreak of the First World War,' he writes in his *Downfall of the Liberal Party* (Collins, 1966), 'initiated a process of disintegration in the Liberal Party which by 1918 had reduced it to ruins.' The crisis for the Liberals during these years was less one of ideology than of leadership. It is true that the party rank-and-file were unhappy about Britain's entry into the war and the way in which it was conducted (censorship, the abandonment of free trade, the drift towards conscription, etc.) but the central episode in the wartime 'disintegration' of the Liberal Party was the formation of Lloyd George's Coalition government in December 1916 with the support of the Labour and Conservative Parties and about half the parliamentary Liberals. Since Asquith and the other half of the parliamentary party – including all the ex-ministers – went into opposition, the Liberal Party was now divided informally into two sections.

At this point, however, the split was not irrevocable. But, in 1917, relations between the two sections worsened, owing to disputes over policy and increasing personal bitterness between the two Liberal leaders. Asquith refused office in the new Coalition: 'Under no circumstances would I serve in a government of which Lloyd George was the head. I had learned by long and close association to mistrust him profoundly . . .' The implications of all this were seen in 1918. Herbert Gladstone, formerly Liberal Chief Whip, wrote:

> The result of 1918 broke the party not only in the House of Commons but in the country. Local Associations perished or maintained a nominal existence. Masses of our best men passed away to Labour. Others gravitated to Conservatism or independence. Funds were depleted and we were short of workers all over the country. There was an utter lack of enthusiasm or even zeal.

The franchise factor

The consequences of the 1918 Reform Act were profound. By giving the vote to women over the age of thirty and removing many of the old technical restrictions on the exercise of the franchise, it trebled the electorate from roughly seven million to 21 million voters. It also introduced important new redistribution clauses which, by creating many new working-class constituencies, almost certainly helped the Labour Party. Thus, for the first time a mass electorate appeared in which the working classes were even more clearly a majority. It was this new democratic electorate that had to be wooed by the politicians in the 1920s in what was essentially a three-party system.

The challenge of Labour

One major aspect of this system after 1918 was the rivalry of the Liberal and Labour Parties for the working-class vote, more especially among first-time voters. It was a contest which the Labour Party won. Labour polled about a third of a million votes in 1910. Its post-war vote steadily increased from 2.3 million in 1918 to 8.3 million in 1929. By contrast, the post-war Liberal vote fluctuated wildly and the party found it difficult to advance consistently beyond its 1910 vote of 3 million. In the 1930s the gap between the two parties widened even further.

The rise of Labour

The fact that, after 1915, the party participated in the Coalition governments on equal terms with Liberals and Conservatives, and Arthur Henderson (Labour's wartime leader) became a member of Lloyd George's small War Cabinet, meant an increase in Labour's power and prestige. At last the Labour Party became a truly independent party.

These years saw an enormous upsurge in trade union membership. Between 1910 and 1914 the trade union force had doubled from roughly two million to four million; between 1914 and 1919 it doubled again to about eight million members – not far off the total today – and the majority of these were in large unions affiliated to the Labour Party. It is this last point that is crucial, for it was these links with the trade union movement, consolidated by the organisational reforms of the new Labour Party constitution of 1918, that gave a vital boost to the Labour Party in terms of finance, organisation and morale during the immediate post-war years. It also helped to give it an established and expanding electoral base among the industrial working class, even though it is fair to add that trade union membership as a whole declined considerably in the later 1920s. Moreover, owing to the existence of full employment and rising wages during the war, the position of the millions of unskilled workers outside the trade unions had improved enormously, and many of them looked with increasing favour upon Labour's promises to defend their gains.

Liberal weaknesses

In all these respects the Liberal Party had nothing comparable to depend upon. In an age of increased class polarisation it lacked any definite class basis or class appeal – 'we are a party of no class', proclaimed Asquith – and this hampered it in a variety of ways. Financially, organisationally, and in terms of electoral appeal, it was in a much weaker position than its Labour rival.

A similar point may be made about policy. The Labour Party now had a much more distinctive programme. The new Constitution of 1918, and the detailed policy statements which accompanied it, offered the party activists the heady vision of a socialist future; while the trade unions gained a definite commitment to large-scale nationalisation, including the railways and the mines. But the Labour Party, particularly under the leadership of MacDonald, tried to be all things to all men. In its immediate social policies – over education, housing, pensions, for example – and its idealistic foreign policy in support of disarmament and the League of Nations, it tried deliberately to woo middle-class voters, especially wavering or disillusioned Liberals. Thus, despite the lip-service paid to socialism in the famous Clause 4 of the New Constitution, Labour in many ways took over rather than displaced Liberal ideology. As Duncan Tanner writes, it 'maintained its roots in a radical Liberal political culture, but made itself a more attractive expression of those sentiments and views'.

But what social and economic policies had the Liberals to offer the working classes to rival the practical and emotional appeal of Labour? They passionately supported free trade, but that was a dying cause, and the Labour Party too were true believers. They were not socialists – but they failed to evolve an industrial policy which could be regarded as a realistic and distinctive alternative to Labour's programme, at least until Lloyd George's support of Keynesian ideas in 1919. Indeed, for most of the 1920s the Asquithian Liberal Party was more mediocre and orthodox in its social and economic ideas than it had been before the war. 'The Radical Liberal thrust', writes Tanner, 'was diminished by apathy, depression and division'.

The post-war world was also less favourable for the Liberals in other ways. The old religious issues with which Liberalism had earlier been identified, such as Welsh disestablishment, were now dead and gone; and Irish Home Rule disappeared from the political agenda. This meant that Irish Catholic voters in Great Britain were no longer in thrall to the Liberal Party; and, like many other British workers, could therefore use their votes to support the Labour Party.

Nor, finally, could the Liberals conteract Labour's practical advantages through the superior appeal of their leaders. Asquith, always remote from working-class experience, was now even more of a back number. Lloyd George, because of his devious industrial policies both during and after the war, had completely lost the confidence of the British labour movement. And Labour had its own charismatic leader in Ramsay MacDonald. Handsome, intelligent, and experienced, MacDonald's vague, emotional style of oratory appealed perfectly to the sentiments of the working-class masses he addressed, and helped to build up amongst many of them an 'undogmatic Labourism' (in Henry Pelling's phrase) which became their established political outlook. Moreover, his earlier anti-war stand (which had cost him his parliamentary seat in 1918) was soon forgiven him in the general tide of disillusionment with the Treaty of Versailles and the realities of 'a land fit for heroes to live in' that typified the early 1920s.

Losing ground to left and right.

MacDonald also had a political strategy. He believed that the key to Labour advance lay, first, in the destruction of the Liberal Party as a rival party on the left and as an alternative government. What Labour had to do, above all, was to retain the lead it had established over the Liberals in 1918, keep them at arm's length, and push them permanently into third place in the electoral stakes. The in-built bias of the electoral system against third parties would then work for Labour, just as it had favoured the Liberals before 1914. Politics would then revolve around a Conservative/Labour struggle in which the Liberals could be presented as an irrelevant and dying party, and Labour as the only possible alternative to the Tories. Ironically, this was a strategy which the Conservative leader, Stanley Baldwin, connived at, since he believed, rightly, that Labour's pressure on the Liberals would push many of the latter's middle-class supporters, fearful of the Labour alternative, into the arms of the Tories.

To the consternation and bewilderment of the Liberals, it was this policy of out-and-out warfare that was applied skilfully and ruthlessly by Labour after 1922, particularly during the period of the first Labour government of 1924 when, despite their absolute dependence on Liberal support in order to survive, the government refused to countenance any pact, alliance, or agreement. As Lloyd George said bitterly (but correctly) at the time:

> Liberals are to be the oxen to drag the Labour wain over the rough roads of Parliament . . . and when there is no further use for them, they are to be slaughtered. That is the Labour idea of cooperation.

Exactly so. The Liberals were slaughtered at the general election of 1924 and reduced to a mere 40 MPs. They lost no less than 105 seats to the Tories, and all the gains they had made in 1923 were completely wiped out. The Conservatives won the election; but Labour, though with 40 seats fewer than in 1923, increased its poll by more than a million votes. Thus, MacDonald had triumphantly secured his major aim – the elimination of the Liberal Party as a major rival on the left. In that sense Labour, no less than the Tories, was the victor in 1924. 'We are', lamented Asquith, 'a dying party, set between the upper and the nether millstones'.

The local dimension

None of this must be taken to suggest that the decline of the Liberal Party was inevitable. Indeed, in the light of recent scholarly work on the period it is impossible to see the whole story of Labour rise and Liberal decline in cataclysmic terms – the pattern was much more fragmented. As Duncan Tanner stresses, after 1918 the Labour Party went on building up its strength in those areas where it had already made gains before 1914: in mining seats, and in Tory working-class areas in London, West Lancashire and the West Midlands. This was due, he argues, not primarily to simple class unity, but to the practical benefits which Labour seemed to offer working people compared with the other political parties – especially a greater emphasis on improving working-class living standards generally. In areas of 'radical' Liberalism, however, such as parts of the Lancashire and Yorkshire textile belt, Labour advance was much more difficult and in rural areas it was virtually non-existent.

Thus, the decline of the Liberal Party was not a steady and continuous process, either chronologically or regionally. The decline in the great industrial and mining areas after 1918 was swift and sharp; in other parts of Britain – particularly in rural areas – it was slow and protracted. Much depended on local factors and their relationship to national issues and party organisation. It is at the local level that the problem of 'Liberal decline' can now be illuminated most convincingly.

Further Reading

Clarke, P. *Lancashire and the New Liberalism* (Cambridge University Press, 1971).

Wilson, Trevor *The Downfall of the Liberal Party 1914–1935* (Collins, 1966)

Tanner, Duncan *Political Change and the Labour Party 1900–1918* (Cambridge University Press, 1990).

Searle, G.R. *The Liberal Party: Triumph and Disintegration, 1886–1929* (Macmillan, 1992).

Turner, John *British Politics and the Great War* (Yale University Press, 1942).

Paul Adelman is the author of several books including *The Decline of the Liberal Party*.

Stuart Ball

The Conservative Dominance 1918–40

The Conservative Party was the dominant force in British politics during the inter-war years, being returned as the largest party in the House of Commons for all but two and a half years.

The Conservative Party has been the most successful force in British politics during the past century, to such an extent that it has often come to regard itself as the natural party of government, and to find defeat and exclusion from power a bitter and divisive experience. The Conservatives have been the largest party in the House of Commons for all but 35 of the years since the Home Rule crisis of 1886. Furthermore, for only 19 of those years has the difference between the Conservatives and their principal rival been more than a mere handful of MPs. The most troubled period in the Conservative Party's modern history was the decade before the outbreak of the First World War in 1914. This was mainly the result of the campaign for tariff reform, which sought a radical reversal of the existing system of trade and taxation in the interests of national regeneration and the preservation of the empire. However, because the policy required the imposition of duties on imports of food which would raise the cost of living and press heavily upon the urban working-class household, it had a catastrophic electoral impact and provoked faction and division within the Conservative ranks. After three consecutive general election defeats, in 1906 and January and December 1910, the Party seemed to be in danger of permanent exclusion from power. At the same time, despite their bitter opposition, the Liberal government was forcing through parliament measures for Irish Home Rule and the dismantling of the Established Church in Wales. In response, the Conservatives moved to the brink of illegal and unconstitutional action, in particular in support of Ulster's refusal to accept the proposed Dublin parliament. Despite by-election successes between 1911 and 1914, it is by no means certain that the Conservatives had broadened their appeal or that the outcome of the general election due by December 1915 would have been a Conservative victory.

Impact of the First World War

The Great War changed everything, and not least the political situation in Britain. Pre-war issues were swept aside, and the new public concerns favoured the Conservatives as the party identified with patriotism, strong defence, and unfettered prosecution of the war. Even before 1914 many Conservatives had advocated conscription, and the Party had little objection to enlarging the directing powers of the state in wartime. This was not the case with the Liberal Party, and this underlay the split between Asquith and Lloyd George in 1916, the event which began the process of Liberal division, disintegration and decline. The Conservatives had entered into an unsatisfactory coalition under Asquith in 1915, but the recast coalition led by Lloyd George between 1916 and 1918 was a genuine political partnership. As the larger force within it, the Conservative Party shared in the credit for winning the war. The general election of December 1918, called immediately after the armistice, was a landslide for the coalition. The Conservatives accounted for 382 of the 523 Coalition MPs elected, whilst only 28 independent Liberals and 63 Labour MPs were returned. The popular mood was anti-German, anti-pacifist, and anti-Asquith: Liberals loyal to Asquith were punished by the voters for the shortages of munitions and the reverses in the early part of the war and for their opposition to Lloyd George in the symbolic Maurice debate of May 1918.

Not only the balance of parties but also the electoral system radically changed. The Reform Act of 1918 introduced a democratic electorate, with the vote for all men at 21 and women at 30. This extension of the franchise to male voters previously excluded is often thought to have assisted the rise of Labour. However, the new male voters were not entirely working class, and even those who were may well have been susceptible to the Conservative appeal, especially in the atmosphere of 'Hang the Kaiser'. This was still more true of women of all classes, enfranchised for the first time in 1918, and during the inter-war period the Conservative Party secured the largest share of the female vote. The Conservatives also benefited from the redistribution of seats which formed part of the 1918 Act. Conservative seats in the home counties with expanding populations were sub-divided to form several new constituencies, whilst many Liberal seats with small electorate's in the west, the north, and in Scotland disappeared. The Conservatives also succeeded in retaining the university seats and the business vote, both of which were overwhelmingly Conservative. Finally, and perhaps most importantly, developments in Ireland removed the solid block of 80 Irish Nationalist MPs who had consistently supported the Liberal Party from the moment Gladstone had taken up Home Rule in 1886. In the general election of 1918 the old Irish party of Parnell and Redmond was swept away by Sinn Fein, but the new MPs refused to take their seats at Westminster, and the seats themselves disappeared in 1922 as a result of the Anglo-Irish Treaty. After the partition, the only Irish MPs in the House of Commons came from the north, and almost all of these were Ulster Unionists who for all practical purposes counted as Conservative MPs. Ireland, so long a barrier to the Conservatives, now became an asset.

Division of the opposition

The general election of 1918 exposed the division of the Liberal Party and hastened its decline. The Conservative Party secured the adherence of few former Liberal ministers or MPs in comparison with the much larger drift to the Labour Party, and the most prominent Liberal to join the Conservatives, Winston Churchill, appeared for many years to be more of a liability than an asset. However, this obscures the fact that at the lower level of Liberal supporters and voters, the benefits were much more evenly divided between the Conservative and Labour Parties. The Liberal decline is too often discussed solely in relation to the rise of the Labour Party: Labour certainly gained former Liberal seats in the larger urban and industrial areas, but in the suburbs, the small towns, and especially in the rural areas, it was the Conservatives who succeeded to the Liberal inheritance. In this they were often assisted by the appearance of Labour candidates who had little chance of winning such seats, but who drew away a portion of Liberal supporters. The struggle between the Liberal and Labour Parties for the left-of-centre in British politics thus appeared greatly to benefit the Conservatives, who won the general election of 1922 with only 38.5% of the popular vote. However, this figure does not take into account the 42 Conservatives returned unopposed or the fact that, despite the repudiation of formal coalition at cabinet level, there were still many informal local pacts with the Lloyd George Liberals in 1922, especially in the north and in Scotland.

In fact, the division on the left of British politics was not a guarantee of success for the right: of the four general elections held during the 1920s, the Conservatives won two and lost two. The two defeats, in 1923 and 1929, occurred when the issues or the public mood did not favour the Conservatives and when they faced a confident Labour Party and a fairly united and effective Liberal Party. On the two occasions when the Conservatives won, the Liberal Party was either still badly divided (in 1922) or through internal wrangling unwilling and financially unable to run a large number of candidates (in 1924). The crucial difference between the massive Conservative victory in 1924 and their defeat at the next election in 1929 lay in the response of Liberal voters. In 1924 many Liberals were influenced by fear of Socialism, and with many constituencies having no Liberal candidate, the Conservatives picked up vital Liberal support. Ironically, the Conservative government's defeat of the General Strike in 1926 meant that by the time of the next general election in 1929, middle-class fear of Labour had considerably lessened. With the Liberals now united under the energetic leadership of Lloyd George, with the propaganda value of his bold plans of public works to reduce unemployment, and with his personal fund financing over 500 candidates, many Liberal voters returned to their old allegiance, and nearly all the Conservative gains of 1924 were lost.

In the election of 1931, the Conservatives were the principal beneficiary firstly of the issues upon which the election was being fought, and secondly of an electoral pact with the Liberals which gave most Conservative candidates a straight fight against a Labour Party which had lost its leader and was in disarray. By the time of the following election in 1935 these two advantages had been diminished but not destroyed. The National government's record in both domestic and foreign affairs was not discreditable, and the coalition still contained half of the Liberal Party (the National Liberals led by Sir John Simon). Although the other half (led by Sir Herbert Samuel) had left the government over the issue of free trade in 1932 and was now in opposition, it was unable to field more than 161 candidates. Some marginal seats were gained by Labour as a result of these Liberal interventions, but too few to make much impression upon the National government's majority: when the results were in, the National government had 429 MPs (of whom 387 were Conservatives), Labour had 154 MPs, and the 'Samuelite' Liberals only 21.

Social basis of Conservative support

At both national and local level, the Conservatives recruited their leadership from the upper class and the upper middle class, of whom by 1918 only a minority supported the Liberal Party, whilst a mere handful supported Labour. These groups provided the Conservative Party with social prestige, traditions of local leadership and public service, and the deferential response that this elicited from many of those in less exalted stations in life. They also furnished the munitions of political warfare: influence, financial backing, the support of the press, and a large supply of prospective candidates who could pay their own way and who were educated, socially respectable and – in most cases – confident enough to perform satisfactorily on the public platform. However, in the age of the mass electorate, the Conservative Party would have withered on the vine had it not also attracted the support, or at least the votes, of much of the lower middle class and a significant number of the work ing class. Indeed, the support of the lower middle class was crucial to the Conservatives. They provided most of the active membership of the Constituency Associations, especially at branch level and amongst the women and the Junior Imperial League, the precursor of the post-war Young Conservatives; this gave the Party a living presence at the grass-roots that money alone could never have created.

At the same time, it is impossible to make sense of the electoral statistics without acknowledging that a substantial portion, around one third, of the various social groups that are lumped together under the shorthand term of 'working class' were intermittent or habitual Conservative supporters. Not once between 1918 and 1940 was the popular vote for the Labour Party larger than that for the Conservatives. The closest Labour came, in their best result in 1929, was 8.38m votes to the Conservatives' 8.65m; on this occasion, the vagaries of the system gave Labour 288 MPs to only 260 for the Conservatives. In all the other general elections between the wars, Labour trailed the Conservatives in votes by between one and five million, and it was not until 1945 that the Labour Party achieved a higher total than their opponents. The causes of working-class Conservatism are as many and varied as those which shape the political outlook of any other group, and it is a grave mistake to dismiss this particular manifestation of popular feeling as having been in some way misguided, mistaken, or merely negative. There were sufficient positive factors to make the Conservative Party a repository of working-class votes: these ranged from the individual combinations of age, relative status, occupation, family and regional traditions, and personal temperament, to the broad appeal of the party to national unity, patriotism, pride in the Empire, independence, self-reliance, and the search for prosperity at home without social upheaval and peace abroad without military adventure. It was not necessary to have a large stake in the world to fear the advent of social chaos or revolution. These themes, many of which were bound up with the economic panacea of tariff reform, run through the posters, leaflets, cartoons, and other propaganda of the Conservative Party, as well as the imagery and rhetoric of Conservative politicians.

Power of the party machine

Although there were areas where Conservatism was weak, and therefore where the party organisation was on a skeleton basis, the party as a whole had an effective presence in all regions and types of constituency. Throughout this period, it ran candidates in almost every seat (making allowance for pacts and coalition partners), and was able to mount a credible challenge in most of them. The strength of the Conservative Party organisation derived directly from the nature and extent of its social support, which provided the two essential components of money and a reservoir of committed voluntary workers. The Conservative Party's greater financial resources at national level, in the form of contributions from individual businessmen rather than from companies, paid for the large staff of party officials, at the Central Office in London and for a regional network of Area Agents. These provided an increasingly elaborate range of support services for the local Associations, including leaflets, posters, publications, professional speakers, and even by the 1930s a fleet of mobile cinema vans. Equally important, the central funds provided grants to help maintain a presence in the poorer constituencies and they assisted with candidates' expenses in the more difficult areas. Most of the safer seats had a well equipped organisation financed by subscriptions from their own MP and the more prominent local supporters. As a result, the majority of constituencies were able to employ a full-time professional agent.

Women had already been involved in voluntary work for the Conservative Party on a large scale through the Primrose League before the First World War. The involvement of women in the Conservative Party between the wars built on this, but it was also due to the facilities which the party provided for social integration in a respectable cause. Conservative women's branches, especially in suburban and rural districts, were not run by working women from shop or factory, but by married women, often middle-aged or older, generally drawn from the middle class, but with upper-class ladies playing the more visible and leading roles. These women had the leisure to engage in a round of social and charitable activities, in which the Conservative Party complemented the Mothers' Union, the Women's Institute, and so on. Women provided the Party with assiduous fund-raisers, with voluntary workers for committee rooms and canvassing, with the organisers of fetes, bazaars, whist drives, and other social functions, but not with leadership. Political discussion was still the prerogative of the numerically much smaller men's branches. By the late 1920s local joint Executive Committees had become the norm in most constituencies, but the chairman and leading figures would still almost invariably be men, as would the candidate. However, this was socially acceptable and seems to have caused little friction. By the end of the 1920s the women's side of the Party was claimed to have over a million members.

The organisational strength of the Conservative Party was a significant factor in its electoral success. Organisation alone cannot win elections if other factors are against a party, but they can help to minimise the scale of a defeat and maximise the margin of a victory. Certainly, the Conservative machine must have had an impact in the marginal seats, where elections are in fact decided. Here the swing of even a few hundred votes for or against can be crucial, and an effective and efficient organisation which can ensure that its own supporters poll in large numbers may make the necessary difference. It is hard to quantify the impact of Conservative strength in this respect, as it was a constant factor throughout the period, but the victory of 1935, in which many Conservatives held on with slim majorities to seats which had been won by Liberals or Labour in 1923 or 1929, might have had a very different outcome without it.

Stanley Baldwin's significance

Conservative governments between the wars were conscious of the need not to appear reactionary, and thus they frequently thwarted the desires of the 'diehards', the contemporary term for the group of right-wing MPs who comprised approximately 20% of the parliamentary party. Constantly aware that they were operating in the context of a mass electorate, Conservative leaders deliberately offered programmes which, whilst distinctive in tone and principle from both the Liberals and Labour, nevertheless would not alarm or alienate middle-class or working-class voters. The personality of Baldwin, leader of the Party from 1923 to 1937, played an important part in this. Baldwin came to prominence in the overthrow of the Lloyd George coalition, and for many he symbolised the victory of honesty and principle over the cynical opportunism which they associated with Lloyd George and his circle. Still more significant was Baldwin's image of moderation. In the face of much Conservative anxiety during the industrial unrest between the end of the war and the General Strike, Baldwin established his authority and his political style by persuading the parliamentary party in 1925 not to support a 'diehard' MP's anti-trade union bill. Baldwin's appeal for industrial harmony and peace between classes created a lasting impression not only upon his audience in the House of Commons but upon the nation at large. In other respects Baldwin also seemed to capture the spirit of the age; the widespread desire for tranquillity at home, peace and disarmament abroad, and a return wherever possible to pre-war verities. Baldwin made highly effective use of the two new forms of media, the radio broadcast and the cinema newsreel. Although from a Worcestershire industrial family, Baldwin deliberately fostered the image of a traditional countryman, who despite his translation to national eminence was as concerned for the welfare of his people as any rural squire would be for his tenants and villagers. He enjoyed widespread popularity with uncommitted, Liberal and even Labour voters. Even after defeat in the general election of 1929 under his own slogan of 'Safety First', he was still acknowledged to be the Party's greatest electoral asset.

Baldwin's style had its drawbacks, and it was only achieved at the cost of frequently thwarting the desires of the Conservative grass-roots: this led to the apathy which partly caused the defeat of 1929, and to the crises over economic policy in 1929–31 and India in 1933–35. On the other hand, under no other Conservative leader would the National government of 1931 have been possible. Baldwin's willingness to sit back and leave formal power to Ramsay MacDonald may have been the result of laziness and lack of resolution, but without it the National government would hardly have lasted for more than a few months. However, with the Conservative Party electorally successful and with such a reassuring figure as Baldwin as its leader, the middle classes felt safe and secure. For this reason fascism failed to make any impact in Britain in the 1930s, as even rebellious Conservatives shunned it and stayed loyal to their party. Nor did the Conservative Party suffer electoral damage from any of the international rifts of the inter-war era. The principal reason for this, and the crucial difference from the Liberal divisions of 1916–24, was that Conservative disagreements were almost never carried to the point of rebel candidatures at general elections, and thus the right-of-centre vote was not fragmented. Even between 1922 and 1924, with the unhealed wounds caused by the fall of the coalition, there was little recrimination in public and no deselections of MPs. This conscious restraint, together with the traditional loyalty to the party (much more than to the leader) and the horror of division, maintained Conservative unity, and internal rancour was rarely permitted to rise to the level where it could help opponents. The greater cohesiveness of the Conservative Party, cemented by its pragmatism on policies, its concentration on the achievement of power as the primary objective, and the breadth and vagueness of its underlying principles, enabled it to surmount these internal strains with surprising ease.

Conclusion

It is easy to look back on British politics between the wars and summarise them as a period dominated by the Conservative Party. However, the Conservative leaders and MPs of the day were never confident that they could secure continued success. In the immediate aftermath of the war the fear of Labour, even of revolution, led to a lack of confidence and to the coalition under Lloyd George. Even after this was abandoned as dangerously counter-productive in 1922, the party remained preoccupied with concern about the likely results of the newly-established 'democracy'. The fickle nature of the new electorate, seen in the 'swing of pendulum' effect against the party in office, also encouraged pessimism about the long-term future of the party. After each victory, within two or three years there were widespread expectations of forthcoming defeat: this was true after the successes of 1918, 1924, 1931 and 1935, and would probably also have occurred after 1922 if Baldwin had not led the Party into disaster a mere 12 months later. It is only when we see the period as a whole that the pattern emerges, and the underlying strengths of the Conservative position begin to show through: for those actively involved in these affairs, they were a constant mixture of achievement and disappointment, in which all too often the past seemed to be unsatisfactory and the future uncertain.

Further Reading

Ball, S. *Baldwin and the Conservative Party: The Crisis of 1929–31* (Yale University Press, 1988).

Close, D.H. 'Conservatives and coalition after the First World War', *Journal of Modern History*, 45, 2 (1973).

Hyde, H.M. *Baldwin* (Hart-Davis MacGibbon, 1973).

Kinnear, M. *The Fall of Lloyd George* (Macmillan, 1973).

Pugh M. 'Popular Conservatism in Britain: continuity and change 1880–1987', *Journal of British Studies*, 27, 3 (1988).

Ramsden, J.A. *The Age of Balfour and Baldwin 1902–40* (Longman, 1978).

Stubbs, J. 'The impact of the Great War on the Conservative Party' and Peele, G. 'Revolt over India' in Peele G. and Cook C. (eds) *The Politics of Reappraisal 1918–39* (Macmillan, 1975).

Thompson, N. *The Anti-Appeasers* (Oxford University Press, 1971).

Williamson, P. 'Safety First: Baldwin, the Conservative Party, and the 1929 general election', *Historical Journal*, 25, 2 (1988).

Stuart Ball is Lecturer in History at the University of Leicester.

PART II
The Locust Years

The inter-war years saw the development of new industries such as chemicals, car-manufacturing, aircraft and light engineering. However, older industries, such as cotton and coal, were in steady decline. The concentration of these industries in particular areas, often to the absence of alternative sources of employment, accounts for the highly localised nature of inter-war unemployment. Traditional responses to such problems in the late nineteenth century had been public works, the encouragement of emigration to the colonies and resettlement on the land at home. All of these ideas continued to crop up in many of the programmes of the inter-war years. However, signs of new thought also began to appear in the 1920s. The ILP's *Socialism in Our Time* in 1926 saw unemployment as the result of slack demand due to under-consumption. The cure, it was argued, was not to cut wages, as was then happening in industry, but to improve working-class incomes, and thus demand, by minimum wages and family allowances. Other works, such as the 1929 Keynes-inspired Liberal 'Orange Book', *We Can Conquer Unemployment*, looked to an immediate programme of public works to achieve the same effect, whilst long-term investment planning was seen as a means of countering future cyclical downturns. In the 1930s maverick Conservatives, such as Harold Macmillan, also began to advocate forms of planning.

Experiments by government, under both Conservatives and Labour, tended to be more limited. The Conservatives, in 1924–29, sought to encourage private investment, but otherwise had few solutions for the growing numbers of long-term unemployed except to suggest their transfer to more prosperous areas. This certainly happened on a considerable scale in the 1920s and 1930s. Workers from South Wales or Durham flocked to the South and Midlands to work in the new industries. These benefited from the introduction of protection after 1932, though not the older export-oriented industries in the blighted regions. The intractability of the problems of these regions led to the designation of 'Special Areas' in 1934 by the Conservative-dominated National Government. These acquired some powers to attract new industries to blighted areas whilst, outside the Special Areas, local authorities like Liverpool and Manchester built airports and trading estates with the same end in view. The impact on unemployment of such activity was, however, strictly limited.

Notices about unemployed marches to London passing through the town were commonplace for much of the local press during the inter-war years. Many of these marches were organised by the National Unemployed Workers Movement, set up by the newly formed Communist Party in 1921. The Communists, however, made few converts amongst the unemployed. Communism made most headway as a critique of monopoly capitalism in the South Wales and Scottish coalfields, and in the East End. Even in these areas it was contained by Labour which, after 1925, sought to exclude Communists from its ranks. The compounding of this exclusion by a Moscow-inspired sectarianism helped to ensure that the Communists ended the 1920s, except in their core areas, on a very low note. It was not until the later 1930s, when the USSR had switched its line and was again encouraging Communist parties to co-operate with other parties of the Left as a way of building alliances against the growing threat of Fascism, that substantial recovery occurred. The most visible means of countering this threat was to take a firm stance on Spain. It was Communist opposition to Franco, more than their work amongst the unemployed, that helped to attract new members in the late 1930s. Even so, in 1939 membership had still only reached 18,000.

The National Government meanwhile adopted a benevolent attitude towards Franco during the Spanish Civil War (1936–39), fearing that his defeat would benefit the Communists. This attitude towards Spain also reflected the policy of appeasement, and particularly the desire to satisfy Mussolini and detach him from Hitler. Appeasement was accompanied, after 1934, by growing rearmament, which not only improved Britain's preparedness for the impending conflict but artificially boosted the economy. Even so, on the eve of the outbreak of the Second World War unemployment was once again over two million.

Derek H. Aldcroft

The Locust Years? Britain's Inter-war Economy

Between the wars Britain saw reasonable economic growth and growing prosperity for much of the population. There was also devaluation, depression, sharp regional contrasts and mass unemployment. Derek Aldcroft explains why.

After a speculative post-war boom, the British economy experienced a sharp but deep slump in 1921 with unemployment levels rising to over two million. The recovery thereafter was somewhat protracted, influenced by the government's policy to return to the Gold Standard at the pre-war parity and then by the 1926 General Strike. The return to gold did not lead to the benefits anticipated by its supporters largely because it overvalued the sterling currency. Hence the boom of the later 1920s was somewhat muted in Britain compared with other countries, especially America. On the other hand, the subsequent depression was less severe than elsewhere, despite the high unemployment levels recorded in 1932. Recovery was also somewhat earlier and more pronounced than in other major countries so that during the cyclical upswing of the 1930s Britain, somewhat exceptionally, was near the top of the growth league table. Yet despite this impressive performance there remained major blackspots. Unemployment remained very high even at the peak of the cycle, while export volumes were well down even on 1913 levels. There was moreover the everlasting problems of Britain's staple industries and depressed areas, neither of which drew much relief from the strong upswing of the period. Only rearmament and war eventually solved these issues.

Post-war boom and slump

Though the pressure of war needs had weakened the economy and checked investment, Britain's economy was not devastated as was the case in so many European countries. In fact, after a temporary lull following the armistice, output and incomes soon regained their pre-war levels and during the years 1919–20, Britain experienced one of the most violent and speculative booms on record. The large pent-up demand for necessities arising from wartime privation and the accumulated balance of liquid resources was partly responsible for the boom. In addition, the early abolition of economic controls, lax fiscal and monetary policies, the strong demand for exports and investment backlogs, accentuated the upswing. But it turned out to be very much a price boom, rather than one of increased output. Wages and prices rose sharply, speculative activity was rife, while total output did not rise significantly. Second-hand assets, especially in the textile and shipping industries, changed hands at vastly inflated prices, with the result that wartime profits were frittered away and many older industries were saddled with debt and overcapitalised.

The boom very soon spent itself and the subsequent collapse was equally dramatic. The origins of the downturn can be traced to a falling off in consumption, tighter monetary and fiscal policies and a fall in exports in the latter half of 1920 as economic conditions deteriorated abroad. By then economic activity was already declining and in the following year Britain experienced one of the worst depressions in history. With the exception of investment, which was bolstered for a time by the public housing programme, all indices of activity fell sharply, and unemployment rose to around 22% of the insured labour force.

1920s: Protracted recovery

Britain experienced a somewhat chequered economic performance during the course of the 1920s. The economy did improve, but it was punctuated by setbacks. There were several factors to explain the relatively poor showing. For one thing, monetary and fiscal policy were constraining, partly because of the aim to get back to the Gold Standard and then the struggle to defend the restored parity which overvalued the currency and hence harmed exports. Secondly, the General Strike in 1926 caused a temporary dip in production. Thirdly, the impact exerted by building and the newer growth industries, such as motor manufacturing, chemicals and electrical engineering, was much less marked than in the case of the United States. Building, for example, collapsed in 1927–28 and in 1926–29 there was a negative growth in construction. Most of the service industries recorded only modest rates of expansion, while the growth rate of the newer industries was no greater than the average for all industry; in any case, their share in total output was still quite small.

The stock explanation, however, is usually cast in terms of exports. Their growth, it is argued, was constrained by high and inflexible wage costs, an overvalued currency and the fact that a large share of Britain's exports consisted of staple products, the demand for which was declining or rising only very slowly. Furthermore, the recovery of European production, together with the development of manufacturing production in many of Britain's former markets outside Europe, curtailed the outlets for British goods. However, too much emphasis should not be placed on the export thesis. The volume of exports actually rose more rapidly than industrial production between 1926 and 1929, though pre-war levels were not regained. The lack of competitiveness argument is also relevant, especially in view of the overvalued exchange rate, but one should bear in mind that given Britain's skewed export structure, it is doubtful whether a lower exchange rate would have made all that much difference to the exports of the staple industries, given the weak international demand for their products.

Whatever the causes of the sluggish performance in the 1920s, it probably helped to soften the impact of the subsequent depression, since the economy did not overshoot itself leaving exhausted sectors in its wake, as happened in America. Hence the chances of a softer landing and an earlier recovery were greater than across the Atlantic.

Impact of the Depression

Britain suffered a lot less severely from the slump of the early 1930s than other major countries, such as Germany and the United States. The declines in consumption and income were quite modest, and even industrial production did not fall as sharply as it had after the post-war boom. Exports, however, declined by more than a third while unemployment rose to over three million at the trough of the cycle, equivalent to some 23% of the insured labour force, though rather less as a percentage of the total labour force.

There were several reasons why the impact was less intense than elsewhere. For one thing Britain had not experienced a very strong boom in the later 1920s with heavy speculation in real estate and share prices, as had occurred in the United States. Secondly, there was no serious collapse of financial institutions in the early 1930s, as in Central Europe and North America. Thirdly, there was a high floor to incomes and consumption throughout the depression years, due to the downward inflexibility of nominal incomes and wages and the strong improvement in the terms of trade. Because the price of food and the price of raw materials which Britain imported fell much more heavily than manufactured prices, there was a significant real income gain for those in work. An additional prop to income was also derived through welfare payments. The effects of these influences on incomes can be seen by the relatively high plateau in residential construction during the depression years. Additionally, late on in the depression, policy action helped to ease the position. Britain left the Gold Standard and devalued the currency in September 1931 which removed the external constraint, while the inauguration of cheap money (i.e. low interest rates) and tariff protection in 1932 helped to relieve the domestic situation.

1930s: Recovery

Recovery of the economy was both earlier and stronger than in many other countries. The United States, France, Belgium, Canada and the Netherlands barely surpassed their former cyclical peaks by the end of the decade. By 1937 Britain had achieved a strong cyclical recovery with income and production levels well above the former peaks of 1929. And although there was a modest downturn in 1937–38, activity resumed its upward trend in 1938–39. However, exports failed to regain previous levels and unemployment still remained a problem, despite a big rise in employment after 1932. In the third quarter of 1937, some 1.4 million people were still without work, that is just over 9.1% of the insured labour force. Much of this residue of unemployment was of a structural rather than a cyclical type. Policy measures have not generally been given much credit for stimulating recovery in Britain. This is true as far as fiscal policy and industrial policy are concerned, but less true with respect to other policy action discussed in the previous section. Recent work has tended to place somewhat greater emphasis than before on the indirect benefits of policy, in particular the removal of the external constraint of a fixed exchange rate provided more room for manoeuvre on the domestic front, for example cheap money and expansion of the monetary base. Tariff protection has also been accorded a more significant role than previously.

Though exports recovered from the low point of the early 1930s they were not the engine of growth in this decade. The recovery was very much a domestically-based one, being powered by housing and the newer industries. Residential construction maintained a high floor during the recession and then advanced sharply through to 1934. The demand for housing was fuelled by falling costs of construction, cheaper borrowing, the liberalisation of building society lending terms, changing tastes and the strength of real incomes. It was in this period that many working-class families entered the housing market for the first time. Expansion of housing and related suburban transport facilities gave a boost to many industries providing furnishings, equipment, consumer durables and the like. At the same time some of the older industries, especially iron and steel and metal bashing, experienced an increase in demand as a result of expansion elsewhere in the economy. The revival of the world economy and later rearmament gave a further life to activity when the consumption-based recovery began to flag.

1921	2,038,000	1922	2,015,000
1923	1,525,000	1924	1,374,000
1925	1,443,000	1926	1,432,000
1927	1,451,000	1928	1,375,000
1929	1,446,000	1930	2,500,000
1931	2,880,000	1932	2,995,000
1933	2,407,000	1934	2,295,000
1935	2,333,000	1936	2,169,000
1937	1,739,000	1938	1,912,000
1939	2,032,000		

Table 1: Unemployment in Britain 1921–39

By the end of the decade the rearmament drive was providing much extra work and even putting pressure on scarce resources.

Unemployment and the regional problem

Unemployment was undoubtedly the major economic and social issue of the inter-war years. It rarely fell below 10% of the insured workforce and in the depression years it reached more than double this figure. A notable feature was the marked disparity in the incidence of unemployment between regions. The north of the country fared very much worse than the south. On average, rates of unemployment in northern counties were at least twice those in the south. For example, while London and the south-east had an average unemployment rate of around 8% between 1929 and 1936, the north-east, north-west and Scotland registered over 20%. Wales was as high as 30%. There were some equally large differences within counties and regions. Chelmsford in the prosperous county of Essex had a rate of only 1.6% in 1937, compared with Pitsea's 36.4%; in the far from prosperous Glamorgan, Resolven recorded only 4.5% as against Ferndale's 48.1%

The heavy geographic concentration of unemployment was largely a product of the north's excessive specialisation on the old export-based staple industries, most of which went ex-growth for one reason or another after the war. These industries were also relatively inefficient and overstaffed and so when market conditions deteriorated they shed labour rapidly. In the first half of the 1920s employment in mining, mechanical engineering, shipbuilding, iron and steel and textiles fell by more than one million. It was these five large groups which accounted for around 50% of the insured unemployed by the end of the decade. A further important factor was the collapse of the export trade. Scotland's problem in particular was largely a product of the dramatic decline in export demand for once staple products. The volume of exports through Scottish ports fell by no less than 56% between 1913 and 1933, and even at the peak of recovery they were still 42% down on the pre-war figure. A similar pattern of events was repeated in other northern regions and in Wales, where in some cases the old staples accounted for 60–70% of the insured labour force. Localised concentrations were even higher, as in the valleys of south Wales and on the north-east coast, where coal and shipbuilding still dominated the landscape. By contrast in the south, with its more favourable locational advantages, the pressure was eased by the rapid growth of newer industries and services trades and extensive residential construction. Some areas in the south were even experiencing shortages of skilled labour by the middle of the 1930s.

Government responses

Government policy was impotent in the face of such a mammoth problem. Not that a great deal was done directly to tackle the issue. There were various *ad hoc* measures of public works, labour migration schemes, industrial reconstruction plans and regional incentives, but these only scratched the surface of the problem. Large-scale programmes of expenditure to activate demand were constrained by conventional economic thought, which emphasised the importance of balanced budgets and external equilibrium, along with the notion that any increase in state spending would simply crowd out private enterprise. In this context the factor of confidence in financial markets, especially in the early 1930s, was of paramount importance. Thus, for much of the period fiscal policy exerted a drag effect on the economy and it was only in the later 1930s, under the impact of defence spending, that the budgetary stance became positively stimulating. More controversially, it was also argued at the time, and reiterated again in more recent literature, that real wages and welfare benefits were too high. The crux of this issue is that employment was lower than it might otherwise have been, because of excessive wage costs, limited regional wage variations to correspond to differing labour market situations, and the high reservation wage, (the benefit to wage ratio which averaged 0.47 for the inter-war years as a whole). Thus unit wage costs remained sticky in the face of weak product prices and relatively low efficiency in the older industries, reducing the demand for labour.

Whether more flexibility in labour markets would have done much to ease the unemployment problem is another matter. Given the structural problems in the northern regions, it is doubtful whether there was any real wage level or exchange rate which could have made the older industries competitive. When capital obsolescence is more or less complete there is virtually no alternative to innovation and structural change. In any case, even if a lowering of wage costs had increased the demand for labour in the staple industries, this would simply have slowed down the pace of structural change. Moreover, from the social point of view, driving down wages and benefits would have left many workers and their families below subsistence existence.

Assessment

For the period as a whole, Britain's overall growth was reasonably respectable, not much different from the long-term trend, although weaker than the performance recorded after the Second World War. Moreover, in the light of the disturbed international conditions during the inter-war years, Britain also did well to escape some of the dramatic upheavals experienced by other countries. Britain did not, for example, suffer the violent inflations which countries such as Germany, Hungary, Poland and Austria experienced in the early 1920s, nor did the banking system disintegrate, as was the case in Central-East Europe and America in the early 1930s. The political system remained remarkably stable compared with that of many countries and there was no lurch to the right of the political spectrum as in Europe during the 1930s. On the other hand, Britain never recovered its former international strength when sterling currency had been 'as good as gold'.

Within British society there were some very striking contrasts. For the majority of workers who remained continuously employed there was a marked rise in living standards, together with the additional benefits of shorter working hours and paid holiday leave which gave access to better and more varied diets, new housing, modern consumer durables and the enjoyment of an increasing range of leisure activities. But for a significant minority without work and for those with large families and/or several dependants on low wages or welfare benefits it was a different story. For these unfortunate individuals the spectre of poverty loomed large; it was a constant struggle to make ends meet and the prospects of any improvement in their situation remained bleak throughout the period. The incidence of poverty and destitution was especially pronounced in the northern regions of the country where the opportunities for employment had much diminished. It contrasted sharply with the growing prosperity of many people in the midlands and the south. This division between north and south and between the old and new – readily captured in much of the contemporary literature as for example, J.B. Priestley's *English*

Journey (1934) – was to plague the British economy for the next half century or more.

Further Reading

Aldcroft, D.H. *The British Economy Between the Wars* (Philip Allan, 1983).
Alford, B.W.E. *Depression and Recovery? British Economic Growth 1918–39* (Macmillan, 1972).
Constantine, S. *Unemployment in Britain Between the Wars* (Longman, 1980).
Garside, W.R. *British Unemployment 1919–39* (Cambridge University Press, 1990).
Peden, G.C. *British Economic and Social Policy: Lloyd George to Margaret Thatcher* (Philip Allan, 1985).
Pollard, S. *The Development of the British Economy 1914–80* (Edward Arnold, 1984).
Stevenson, J. *British Society 1914–45* (Penguin Books, 1984).
Williams, L.J. *Britain and the World Economy, 1919–70* (Fontana/Collins, 1971).

Derek H. Aldcroft is Professor of Economic History at the University of Leicester and visiting Professor at the Anglia Polytechnic University.

Margaret Morris

The General Strike

Was the General Strike a watershed in the history of the labour movement?

'It was a great **class** demonstration . . . It will undoubtedly go down in history as the most wonderful working-class event of our day,' wrote A.A. Purcell, one of the members of the TUC General Council just after the General Strike was called off. Yet Beatrice Webb, leading socialist intellectual and social reformer, dismissed it contemptuously as 'a nine days' wonder'. Fifty years later, historians were equally divided in their assessment of the place of the General Strike in British history, as illustrated by two of the many books published in 1976:

> 1926 proved to be a turning point in the development of the working-class movement: it marked the end of the last great period of working-class militancy and it saw a massive shift in the outlook and orientation of the trade union movement. (Martin Jacques)

> Any event as dramatic in character as the General Strike can readily be viewed as a historical watershed. The difficulty of seeing the crisis of 1926 in this light has, however, already been indicated . . . only in a very modest and unspectacular fashion, therefore, did the General Strike alter the ideas or the behaviour of the union movement. (G.A. Phillips)

The working class betrayed?

In attempting an evaluation of these different perceptions it would seem logical to begin with establishing the aim and results of the 1926 strike. The General Strike was about a dispute in the coal industry but the miners themselves were not on strike in 1926: they were locked out by the coal-owners who were determined to impose wage cuts, longer hours and local negotiations. The strike was called by the TUC to show solidarity with the miners but it was called off before achieving anything. This disappointing outcome was at the heart of the most bitter contemporary dispute of all: whether the General Strike had been 'betrayed' by the members of the General Council, as many of the rank and file strikers believed. The Council members, however, even those regarded as militant like George Hicks of the Building Workers, took a common stand in defending their own actions:

> My colleagues on the General Council are certainly not all 'fools and traitors'. And I have not suddenly been bereft of my senses or suffered the loss of my integrity. I exercised the same faculties, the same tact and judgement during the General Strike as I have done in the other positions I have occupied.

The problem for almost all the trade union leaders in May 1926 was that they did not believe in political strikes. They owed their prominence to their negotiating skills and saw their role as maintaining and controlling their own unions, and advancing or defending the wages and conditions of their members by whatever means seemed appropriate at the time. This could include leading a strike but they were cautious about the use of the strike weapon and very aware of both the hardship that strikes could cause their members, and the drain on union funds. Militancy had been successful in 1919 and 1920, but nearly all the unions had been forced on to the defensive in the recession of 1921–23 and union membership nationally had fallen from 8.3 million in December 1920 down to 5.4 million.

The trade union leaders were very close to the leaders of the Parliamentary Labour Party both ideologically and through daily contact. A quarter of the members of the General Council were MPs, and several had served in the 1924 Labour government. They saw a clear distinction between what could be achieved by trade union action and what should be done through Parliament. In 1919 and 1920 there had been a searching debate in the whole labour movement over the validity and potential effectiveness of 'Direct Action' (ie. political strikes). This had ended with a victory for constitutionalism. In his memoirs, J.R. Clynes, General and Municipal Workers Union and Lord Privy Seal in the 1924 Labour government, wrote:

> No General Strike was ever planned or seriously contemplated as an act of Trade Union policy. I told my own union in April that such a step would be a national disaster, and a fatal step to Union prestige.

The Labour leader, Ramsay MacDonald, was strongly opposed to such strikes and thought they could damage the electoral prospects of the Labour Party.

There were other attitudes, however, within the trade union movement. In particular, the communist-influenced National

Minority Movement was increasing its support and other, younger militants such as Ernest Bevin were so disappointed by the record of the 1924 Labour government that they were prepared to use trade union strength to protect the working class rather than wait for the next election. Certainly, solidarity as a means of mutual support in industrial disputes had widespread support. It was recognised that the miners as the largest and economically most powerful group of workers were at the forefront of trade union struggle and that if the coal-owners could force them to accept large wage cuts other employers would follow suit. The memory of the failure of the Triple Industrial Alliance to help the miners in 1921 was ever present, and a powerful inducement for some action to be taken. The success of 'Red Friday' in July 1925, when the government agreed to subsidise the coal industry for nine months while a Royal Commission looked into ways to modernise the industry, increased confidence among all trade unionists, both those who put their faith in industrial action and those who counted on negotiations and the role of Prime Minister Baldwin as the umpire who would ensure 'fair play'.

A last-minute decision

Most of the General Council clung on to their hope that something would be worked out by the Samuel Commission until the last minute. As a result, it was not until three days before the subsidy ran out and the coal owners were due to impose their lock-out that the TUC took any decisions about how it should go about helping the miners. The General Council did not have power to commit its constituent unions to a strike, but a conference of Executives was called and a Ways and Means Committee was set up headed by A.A. Purcell and Ernest Bevin. After considering such limited action as a two-hour electricity blackout, the Committee under Bevin's influence proposed an indefinite solidarity strike on a very large scale involving most, although not all, of the country's key industries. The Executives gave an overwhelming vote of support.

The next few days saw an upsurge of activity in preparation for the beginning of the strike. At rank and file level, there was unprecedented enthusiasm and commitment, leading to an almost total stoppage in the industries asked to come out. The TUC did not want to harm the community so essential services such as domestic electricity or sewage and rubbish collection were maintained. The aim was to bring industry to a standstill and so put pressure on other employers and the government to intervene with coal-owners. The TUC General Council insisted that this was a 'national' solidarity strike and not a 'general' ie. political, strike but the more cautious among them were deeply worried from the outset about what they were doing. In so far as cutting wages was integral to bringing down costs, which was part of government policy for making British exports competitive while maintaining the Gold Standard at its historically high level, it had to be faced that the strike involved a political challenge. It was also seen by Baldwin as a personal challenge to his status as a mediator. He was determined that he would not negotiate until the strike was unconditionally called off.

Attempts to compromise

As this began to be understood by the General Council many of them felt out of their depth. They had seen the threat of the strike as a form of pressure and had hoped that it would not be necessary to call it. Not only had their bluff been called, but they were faced with accusations that the strike was illegal from Sir John Simon, who told the House of Commons that the trade union leaders would be liable 'to the utmost farthing' of their possessions. They were worried too that the strike might fall into the hands of the Communist Party or, alternatively, collapse. Although there is no evidence that either of these two worries was justified, they put great pressure on the TUC to look for a way out. In their scenario all strikes had to end in a settlement and the issue was only whether the compromise would be the best that could realistically be achieved.

The difficulty was that it was not their own dispute, and they failed to grasp the utter determination of the coal-owners to push through their policy without compromise. Instead of appreciating this, they directed their attention to the leaders of the Miners' Federation and urged them to be less intransigent. The miners were more prepared to make concessions than they were willing to admit in public, but they wanted reassurance that the coal-owners had been nailed down before committing themselves.

There was a long-standing personality clash between A.J. Cook, secretary of the Miners' Federation, and J.H. Thomas of the NUR. This became a very serious cause of distrust between the miners and the TUC when Thomas took over the negotiations. Sir Herbert Samuel, chairman of the Royal Commission, was drawn in to help prepare a compromise document. He insisted that he had no mandate from the government to act as a go-between but largely through the influence of Thomas, the General Council persuaded themselves that if the strike was called off Baldwin would ensure that agreement was reached along the lines of the Samuel Memorandum.

Later Ernest Bevin admitted that the Council 'made the biggest bloomer' over the Samuel Memorandum, but at the time the Council put the blame on the miners for not accepting it and so leaving Baldwin with an excuse for not seeing that it was implemented. Even within their own terms, criticism can be levelled at the Council for not taking longer to pin down the possibilities of a compromise before calling off the strike. It may be that no better outcome could have been achieved as both Baldwin and the coal-owners were adamant: the coal-owners against a national settlement of any sort and Baldwin against giving encouragement to the use of the General Strike as a weapon of political pressure. Nevertheless, it is easy to understand why the mass of strikers who had sacrificed their wages and thrown themselves into the organisation of the strike felt let down. There was widespread middle-class sympathy for the miners as well as an outstanding act of solidarity by the working class and many were convinced that some better outcome should have been possible.

Conclusion

The General Strike remains a unique event but there are many reasons for being cautious about judging the part it played in the history of the period. First, it is not possible to isolate the effects of the strike from those of the mining lockout, which dragged on until November and prevented normal working in many industries. Secondly, it is difficult to separate developments arising out of the strike from the effects of mass unemployment and the structural changes taking place in British industry. Thirdly, the government's action in carrying through the 1927 Trade Disputes and Trade Union Act had a vital bearing on relations between the parliamentary and trade union wings of the movement in the aftermath of the strike. Although there was a breach between many of the rank and file trade unionists and the official leadership, the Trade Disputes Act brought the trade unions and Labour Party closer together and helped to ensure the election of the 1929 Labour government. Finally, before there had been time to recover from and reassess the experiences of 1926, they were overlaid by the failures of that government, by the world slump and the rise of Fascism, so that while it is possible to talk of the immediate and long-term effects of the strike, there is a void in the medium term: the General Strike very rapidly became 'old history'.

Margaret Morris is Director of Modular Programmes at Guildhall University.

Andrew Thorpe
The 1931 Crisis

Why did 1931 prove so disastrous for the Labour Party? Andrew Thorpe explodes some myths.

It would be difficult to think of any other event in modern British political history which has been the subject of so many myths, counter-myths and, occasionally, barefaced lies as the crisis which gripped the nation between August and October 1931.

The basic outlines seem clear enough. The minority Labour government, which had been elected to office in May 1929 but which had since presided over a worsening economic and financial position, was faced with the urgent need to balance the budget and so restore foreign confidence in the integrity of the nation and its currency, necessary if Britain was to remain on the Gold Standard. The choice eventually resolved itself into whether or not to cut unemployment benefit by 10%. When the cabinet split, unable to agree to a fundamental attack on one of the basic tenets of the Labour Party since its inception – the right to 'work or maintenance' – the Prime Minister, Ramsey MacDonald, was forced to offer the government's resignation. However, he then stayed on as head of a 'National government', which included few Labour followers but which included and was supported by Conservatives and Liberals. Ultimately the Gold Standard could not be held, but the new government nonetheless decided to fight a general election as a single entity under MacDonald, and duly won by the largest majority in British electoral history, with 554 seats to Labour's 46. It used to be argued that this was the result of some dark conspiracy of anti-Labour forces engineered by MacDonald eager for the kisses of duchesses, or by bankers keen to destroy a 'socialist' government; that the election, in particular, had been, in the words of the *Manchester Guardian*, 'the most fraudulent of our times'. This was the orthodox view for many years. Yet it was almost totally at variance with the facts.

Politics 1929–31

The second Labour government elected in 1929 began well enough. Its leading figures, MacDonald, Philip Snowden (Chancellor of the Exchequer), Arthur Henderson (Foreign Secretary) and J.H. Thomas (Lord Privy Seal) were experienced and widely respected. Early foreign policy successes were capped by MacDonald becoming the first British Prime Minister to address the United States Congress. At home, moves were made to put in place some of the reforms that Labour had promised in its ambitious election manifesto.

After this bright start, however, things began to fall apart. The onset of a world depression towards the end of 1929 meant that unemployment rose from 1.1 million to 2.8 million during the government's life. There were conflicts with the trade unions over this and over the failure to introduce reforms the unions wanted. The left of the party began to break away in protest, with the resignation of and formation of the New Party by Sir Oswald Mosley, and open rebellion among Independent Labour Party MPs (still nominally part of the Labour Party). Jewish and Catholic voters were alienated by government policy over Palestine and Church schools. From 1930 onwards, the party was faring abysmally in by- and local elections, and by the early summer of 1931, it had no prospect of anything but crushing defeat at the next election.

The Liberals had been forced into supporting the government in Parliament by the refusal of the Conservative leader, Stanley Baldwin, to negotiate with them after the 1929 election. But this created difficulties for an already enfeebled party. Their leader, David Lloyd George, was unpopular with many MPs, as was his line of supporting the government in Parliament. And although they had fought on a radical employment-creation policy in 1929, many Liberals had not really believed that it could work, and as economic crisis mounted they returned increasingly to first principles: to preserve free trade and to cut public expenditure. But free trade was losing popularity, and 'economy' was also the cry of the Conservatives by early 1931. The party had little money and declining organisation, and fared abysmally in those by-elections it could manage to fight. From late 1930 onwards right-wing Liberals like Sir John Simon were talking to the Conservatives about a possible defection: and although such moves came to little at the time, they clearly presaged the way the Liberal Party was moving. One hope was electoral reform, but although the Labour government reluctantly agreed to introduce a bill as the price of continued Liberal support, it would almost certainly have been blocked by the Conservative-dominated House of Lords, even if it had been able to pass the Commons.

Meanwhile the Conservatives had had their problems too. The increasing economic crisis convinced more and more people that protective tariffs on imports were necessary, but Baldwin was cautious, having lost the 1923 election on the issue. This led to discontent with his leadership, and numerous crises. But the party finally committed itself to protection in October 1930; Baldwin saw off a renewed challenge to his leadership the following March; and by early summer 1931 the party was winning by-elections, and was substantially united around a policy package of economy, protection and imperial preference, and assistance to the agricultural voters whose defections had cost the party dear in 1929. They were poised on the brink of success in a general election which could not be long delayed. The way it came, though, was totally unexpected.

The August crisis

In February 1931 the House of Commons had set up a committee on national expenditure under the businessman Sir George May, to investigate and make recommendations on measures to meet the growing budget deficit. When it reported at the end of July, it predicted a deficit of £120 million and recommended cuts of £96 million and increases in taxation totalling £24 million. The cabinet set up a committee of ministers to deal with it and dispersed for its holidays. However, a financial crisis had been brewing in Europe since the collapse of the Austrian Credit Anstalt early in the year, and by July bankers were in a heightened state of nervousness. The May report, therefore, led to a severe crisis of confidence in sterling. The cabinet's economy committee was called back for emergency meetings which agreed to cuts totalling 78 million, which it believed would meet the situation. When these were put to the full cabinet on 19 August, however, the latter would only agree to cuts of 56 million; and the bankers, the opposition leaders (who had to be consulted, given that with Labour a minority government their support would be necessary to get any proposals through Parliament) and MacDonald and Snowden did not believe that this would be sufficient to restore confidence. But the TUC, vital if the Labour movement was to be kept together, refused at a meeting on 20 August to accept any cuts at all, and many ministers, while prepared to stand up to the TUC, were not prepared to be dragged along at the heels of the Conservatives and Liberals. By 22 August, Henderson had emerged as the leading opponent of further cuts. However, the cabinet authorised further appeals for loans to be made to the American bankers on a hypothetical basis: if unemployment benefit was cut by 10% would they assist the government? The following evening they got their reply: if the cut was made, they would receive the money. This was not, as so often alleged by Labour people at the time and since, 'dictation' or a 'bankers' ramp'. Far from it. The bankers had been asked their advice, and had given it, just like the TUC. Still, it put ministers on the spot. By a margin of 11 to 9 they voted for a cut, but the minority was too large and powerful to allow the government to go on. MacDonald took the government's resignation to King George V, but the latter knew that the opposition leaders, Baldwin and Samuel (acting instead of the ill Lloyd George) would support a national government under MacDonald, and asked the Premier to stay on. MacDonald then saw the opposition leaders, who were also keen for him to stay; and the following day (24 August) he told his Labour colleagues that he would be doing just that. Four members of the cabinet supported him, and three – Snowden, Thomas (now Dominions Secretary) and Lord Sankey (Lord Chancellor) – came into the new cabinet, which also included four Conservatives and two Liberals.

MacDonald's motives have been much discussed. But it seems that a combination of a clear sense that his duty was to solve the crisis, loyalty to a monarch who had personally asked him to stay on, encouragement from the opposition leaders, and anger at what he saw as the irresponsible attitude of his erstwhile colleagues and the TUC, were the important considerations. Even so, he stressed that the government was to be temporary only and that there would be no election appeal by the National government as such. Why did this change?

From National Government to general election

There is no need to doubt that MacDonald was being honest when he told his former colleagues that there would be no election. He believed the new governemnt would balance the budget and save the Gold Standard, and then dissolve so that an election could be fought on party lines. This was the overwhelming view among Conservatives, too. However, within six weeks an election had been called. Why?

One reason was that the members of the new government found that they could work well together. The Liberals had no problems. It was decided that there would be no interference with free trade before an election, and so a major potential area of conflict with the Conservatives was removed. MacDonald and Baldwin found working together congenial; in particular Baldwin, effectively deputy Prime Minister, had power but could hide behind MacDonald, who for his part was relieved to be in a less difficult environment. The Conservatives, more generally, came to realise that their National allies might not be a block to protectionalist policies after all; true, Snowden (who remained Chancellor) was a free trader, but he had just announced that he would be retiring from the Commons at the next election, and MacDonald and Thomas were known to be converts to tariffs. In addition, the Liberals were known to be on the verge of a split. Simon and other MPs had no objection to tariffs and would be happy to take the place of Samuel's free trade supporters if it came to it. But the situation within the Labour Party was also a consideration.

Labour had gone into opposition on 24 August believing that it was in a strong position. It had condemned all cuts, and believed that this would make it popular. It elected Henderson, a senior and powerful figure, as its leader. But things were soon going wrong. Henderson was an ineffectual and uninspiring leader. Freed from office, the party swung to the left, stopped thinking about detailed policy, and called airily instead for 'socialism' without any clear idea of what it meant. And as revelations began to be made of the extent to which Labour ministers had agreed to cuts – in, for example, the salaries of employees in the public sector, like teachers – then their potential support and credibility crumbled. As Conservative pressure for an election grew, hardly abated by the fact that Britain was forced off gold on 21 September as a result of a renewed sterling crisis, Labour leaders became increasingly pessimistic. Though putting a brave face on things in public, they were expecting the loss of around 100 seats by the time the election was called.

All this was greatly encouraging to the government. By the end of September, having passed the cuts, it was seeking a basis on which it could fight an election as a united body, although the Conservatives were keen to ditch Samuel's free trade Liberals and replace them with the followers of Simon. They failed in the latter, however, because MacDonald was keen to retain as many non-Conservatives as possible, so as not to appear a Tory puppet, and because Samuel saw nothing but doom for the Liberals if, in a national crisis, they abandoned the government. The problem was tariffs. But on 5th October it was agreed that there would be no government manifesto as such; each party within the government would put forward its own line, but MacDonald would issue an appeal of his own for a 'Doctor's Mandate' to investigate any and every possible way of restoring Britain's deteriorating balance of trade. This meant, of course, that the National parties could rule out no solution in advance. Thus the government agreed to fight an election, and Parliament was formally dissolved on 7 October, with polling set for 27 October.

The election campaign

The election campaign has been the subject of myth-making. Labour supporters often attribute the party's defeat to a series of stunts and scares. These certainly took place. MacDonald and other National candidates brandished German banknotes from the inflationary period of the early 1920s, warning that the same would happen if Labour came to power. Runciman argued that the Labour government had become so insolvent that the money of 9 million or so small savers with the Post Office savings bank had been at risk. This was all so much nonsense. But to claim that it was responsible for Labour's defeat was just as ridiculous (and in any case the Labour press and candidates often got up to much the same sort of thing).

As we have seen, Labour's expectations at the start of the campaign had been grim, and the campaign merely exacerbated its difficulties. The ex-ministers found it impossible to counter the charge that they had run away at a time of grave national crisis. Their now widely-known support for cuts while in government, and subsequent rejection of the need for any cuts when in opposition, suggested political dishonesty. Their attempt to play on the anger of the unemployed at the benefit cut by promising its immediate restoration backfired. Many workers wanted jobs, not benefits, and the Labour campaign singularly failed to suggest how more work might be created. Indeed, the record of the second Labour government, in more than doubling unemployment in just over two years, was a considerable handicap, lumbering the party with an image of misery and depression which was to dog it for years. Also, Labour did not promise immediate restoration of pay cuts in the public sector; they would only be raised again when the economic situation allowed. But this was no more than the government was promising. In desperation, Labour candidates resorted increasingly to appeals for 'socialism' and for the defence of free trade. But no-one really knew what they meant by 'socialism', least of all themselves, and free trade was no longer popular after the troubles of the previous two years. Well before polling only the most fervent Labour partisan seriously expected anything but crushing defeat.

On the other hand, the government had considerable positive appeal. The 'National' tag suggested it was in some way above mere 'party'. MacDonald and his National Labour colleagues were raised to heroic status. And, following the departure from gold, exports became cheaper, while the formation of the National government probably led to a mild increase in business confidence, with the result that unemployment was falling from mid-September until the end of the year, not by massive amounts, but by enough to suggest that the corner had been turned. The lesson seemed plain: the National government would cut unemployment whereas Labour had increased it. And here the Conservatives, who comprised the bulk of National candidates, came into their own. Their package of proposals seemed to offer the chance of more prosperity; in particular, protection was very popular indeed. Whereas Labour wanted to wait for socialism, and the Liberals could only suggest international cooperation to improve matters, the Tories had a policy which could be implemented straight away and which might just work. The vast majority of Conservative candidates were not just openly admitting their protectionism, they were shouting it from the rooftops. Its popularity merely confirmed that even without the National government they would have won an overwhelming victory at the next election after 1929.

Labour had hoped that the government might fall apart during the campaign but, in fact, the Conservatives and their allies got on reasonably well. Of course there were hiccups in some places, with Conservatives and Liberals fighting each other, but these were not typical. By the close of polling few politicians had much doubt about who would win; but very few were expecting the scale of the victory about to be announced.

Results and aftermath

In fact, the National government won 554 seats (including 470 Conservative, 35 Simonites, 33 Liberals and 13 National Labour) and Labour only 46 (the ILP won 6 seats). In terms of the numbers of votes cast, Labour had not done so badly, but even so, the government had won 67.2% of the votes to its 29.3% (a fall from 37.1% in 1929). The government had won seats almost everywhere, even in rock-solid Labour areas like Sheffield, Attercliffe and Bermondsey (where the defection of Catholic voters, as elsewhere, was undoubtedly a factor). Labour had been driven back to its heartlands: and few they were. More than half the MPs sat for mining seats, and most of the rest came from the slum areas of London. No seats at all had been won in Sheffield, Manchester, or Birmingham. The only ex-cabinet minister to save his seat was George Lansbury; he became leader. And failure at the next election was almost assured from the outset. For Labour to win a majority then it would have taken a swing of 20% from the Conservatives; and that was never likely to happen. In fact, the National government won the 1935 election by a large majority and looked set to win the election after that, which had to be postponed because of the outbreak of the Second World War.

That is not to say that the National government did not face problems in the years ahead. In 1932 the Samuelite Liberals objected to protection when it was introduced. They were persuaded not to resign, but they did so in September over imperial preference. By then, their departure caused hardly a stir. MacDonald remained Premier until 1935, when he was succeeded by Baldwin; but the real strong man of the government was Neville Chamberlain, appointed Chancellor of the Exchequer after the election, who eventually became Prime Minister in 1937. It would take the dark days of 1940 to remove him, and to install in power a more wide-ranging Coalition under Churchill.

Conclusion

That Coalition, and the war, were to help bring Labour back to office in 1945, but before then, partly as a result of the events of 1929–31, it was never remotely close to taking power. This was not really due to the events of 1931, however. Labour had entered office in 1929 but had promised a great deal, and, in the event, too much. Not only could it not fulfil its promises, it was also faced with a deteriorating economic situation with which it was in no way equipped to deal. By mid–1931 it was facing a defeat which, though unlikely to be on the scale of that which ultimately occurred, would nonetheless have forced it out of office for years to come. The Liberals, likewise, were in dire straits by mid–1931 and would also have been dealt a crushing blow, and have split, regardless of the events of the late summer and autumn of that year. Thus the events of the 1931 crisis were not a plot to oust a successful Labour government, nor an aberration which wrenched British politics from one path to another. They were simply an exaggerated and unexpected development of already existing trends.

Andrew Thorpe is Lecturer in History at the University of Exeter.

Andrew Mitchell
Mosley and the BUF

Who supported fascism in Britain in the 1930s? Andrew Mitchell examines the background to and development of the British Union of Fascists.

Fascism usually conjures up images of Nazi Germany or Mussolini's Italy but, in the inter-war period, several British fascist groups also emerged. The most significant was the British Union of Fascists (1932–40), founded and led by Oswald Mosley (1896–1980), a minor aristocrat. Previously, Mosley had been both a Tory and an Independent MP as well as a minister in the 1929–31 Labour government.

Mosley's road to fascism

Mosley's fascism was rooted in the First World War and its aftermath. His wartime experiences, in the Royal Flying Corps, the trenches and government service, made him despise the prewar political system and its inability to maintain peace. He felt that Lloyd George's executive approach to wartime organisation and the military ideals of obligation, self-sacrifice and collective purpose could create a better post-war society. Therefore, Mosley entered politics in 1918 to prevent another conflict and build a new society, based on economic progress and social justice, which would honour the 'war generation'.

However, Mosley's involvement in mainstream politics between 1918 and 1931 alienated him from the parliamentary system. His 'new Britain' failed to materialise due to international and domestic economic constraints, the 1920–21 downturn and the dominance of orthodox financial thinking. Elected as a Coalition Unionist MP in 1918, Mosley soon became disenchanted with the lack of reform and the resurgence of pre-war political attitudes and practices. In 1920 he abanboned the Coalition and, until 1924, sat as an Independent. From 1923, Mosley formulated unorthodox ideas to revitalise the British economy and combat unemployment (over 1 million throughout the 1920s, rising to nearly 3 million in the 1929–32 depression). Conventional deflationary policies and the restoration of the pre-war Gold Standard were rejected by Mosley, who emphasised increasing domestic demand, providing public works and developing imperial resources.

He joined the Labour Party in March 1924, assuming that socialism in office would unveil far-reaching economic and social reforms. Yet, in power, both the Conservatives and Labour pursued orthodox economic policies. As Chancellor of the Duchy of Lancaster (1929–30), Mosley discovered Labour would not countenance radical measures to cope with the mounting economic crisis. He resigned from office in May 1930 when the government rejected his reflationary 'Mosley Memorandum' which pressed for national reconstruction based on a 'war cabinet', a protected home market and a £200 million public works programme. After failing to carry his proposals at the October 1930 party conference, Mosley left Labour in February 1931 to form the New Party.

His maverick parliamentary career fostered the illusion that individual talent out-weighed party commitments. Moreover, Mosley's capacity to inspire devotion and generate popular approval through platform oratory also led him to underestimate the institutional nature of modern political power and support. These misconceptions reinforced his self-confidence and encouraged a disregard for the political 'rules of the game'.

The New Party, founded in March 1931, aimed to circumvent establishment conservatism and introduce radical policies to reverse Britain's economic decline. It also revealed Mosley's growing acceptance of fascism. The party advocated a largely unchecked executive which would expand the home market through planning, protection and public works. Mosley responded to the militant left's violent reaction to the New Party by creating a youth squad (Nupa) to safeguard meetings and to resist any attempted left-wing coup in a national emergency. At the October 1931 general election though, the New Party, unsuccessfully fielding 24 candidates, was crushed. Convinced that the old order was bankrupt and disintegrating, Mosley embraced fascism to remedy Britain's decline and frustrate perceived communist designs on power. Visits to Mussolini and Nazi leaders in January 1932 strengthened his faith in fascist politics.

BUF: Politics and violence

Mosley formed the British Union of Fascists (BUF) on 1 October 1932. The BUF's programme, outlined in his book The Greater Britain (1932), constituted the most coherent European fascist analysis, although from 1934 its presentation became cruder and distinctly anti-semitic. To rejuvenate the nation, the movement called for a fascist executive subject to few restraints, a corporate state and a self-sufficient imperial bloc to surmount the 'parasitic' international economy. The BUF also proposed non-involvement in overseas affairs which, in its view, did not directly affect British interests. With its blackshirt uniforms, marches and rallies, the BUF was heavily influenced by continental fascism, but Mosley considered it an authentic 'British' response to national problems which sought power by constitutional methods. Initially, the movement set up defence forces in London and elsewhere to protect blackshirt meetings and to prepare for the expected economic collapse when fascism would save the country from communism.

Between January and July 1934, Lord Rothermere, the Tory press baron, covered BUF activities sympathetically in the *Daily Mail*, raising membership to an estimated 50,000. Rothermere mistakenly saw the blackshirts as the embodiment of robust conservatism. During this period, the BUF also attempted, without much success, to penetrate the establishment through the January Club (a dining forum), the civil service and various educational institutions.

The BUF provoked a strident reaction from communists and other left-wingers who observed that fascism abroad had destroyed labour organisations and basic freedoms. Disturbances resulted from the interaction of these opposed political forces. Anti-fascists disrupted blackshirt meetings to muzzle the BUF and erode its morale and public image. In this antagonistic climate, Mosley addressed 10–12,000 people at London's Olympia in June 1934. The spoiling tactics of anti-fascists present sabotaged his speech and blackshirt stewards replied with forcible ejections and assaults. For the public, Olympia symbolised fascist violence and, afterwards, Hitler's 'Night of the Long Knives' hardened anti-BUF sentiment. These developments led Rothermere, already repudiating the movement's dictatorial, anti-semitic and corporate tendencies, to withdraw his press support. Consequently, membership fell to around 5,000 by October 1935.

After Olympia, the BUF laid greater stress on electoral politics since the receding depression diminished the prospect of securing power through a crisis. Accordingly, reforms were introduced in 1935 to centralise control and remodel the organisation along constituency lines. The BUF boycotted the 1935 general election because this overhaul was incomplete, but later selected 81 constituencies for the next election and announced prospective candidates. From mid–1934, to recover support, the fascists offered various interests economic protection and corporate representation. For example, ailing northern industries were targeted and petty bourgeois occupations defended against big business competition. Similarly, anti-exploitation propaganda wooed unorganised labour. Single-issue campaigns were also employed, including the 'Mind Britain's Business' platform during the 1935 Abyssinian crisis and the 'Back the King' policy concerning the 1936 abdication controversy.

Anti-semitism

The BUF's infamous anti-semitic campaign from late 1934 was central to revival efforts. From the beginning, anti-semitism permeated the movement, but now it became increasingly pronounced. In part, this represented a cynical attempt to boost membership by playing on anti-Jewish prejudice. BUF views on finance, business and communism also engendered hostility towards Jews, as did the need to sustain the activist 'core' during lean times. Militant Jewish activity, motivated by German events and including assaults on blackshirts, was an additional contributory factor. Mosley's Albert Hall speech in October 1934 detailed his opposition to Jewry. Jewish dominance in business and international finance, he maintained, had suppressed fascist growth and endangered the national economy. Jews were also condemned for attacking fascists and overwhelming the native culture of certain districts. Finally, Mosley claimed the Jews had no national loyalties and desired intervention against Nazi Germany.

Anti-semitic propaganda struck a chord in London's East End. Facing unemployment and housing problems, this depressed region possessed both anti-immigrant traditions and areas of concentrated Jewish settlement and economic activity. The BUF attracted lower middle and working-class support by pinning the blame for East End conditions mainly on the 'exploitative' practices of Jewish businesses, employers and landlords there. East London branches were set up between 1934 and 1936 and blackshirt resources were poured into the area. The fascist presence generated increasing attacks on Jews, their property and communists in the mid–1930s. Local Jewish, communist and worker elements formed opposition groups and ignored official policies of non-engagement. Violence flared from the convergence of these forces. At the 'Battle of Cable Street' on 4 October 1936, Mosley's intended East End march with 2–3,000 blackshirts was blocked by a gathering of 100,000 communist-led anti-fascists. After the police had banned the march, the fascists travelled westwards and dispersed peacefully. But police clashes with anti-fascists produced 83 arrests and over 100 casualties. Just days later, fascist youths unleashed the 'Mile End Road Pogrom', damaging Jewish property and assaulting people regarded as Jews.

To stem this violent tide, the government introduced the Public Order Act of January 1937. The latter reflected concern over the East End and aimed to counter extremist threats to public order by strengthening police powers. This legislation outlawed political uniforms, enabled the police to ban local marches and prevented the stewarding of outdoor meetings. The use of insulting words in public speeches was also prohibited. Although the Act helped to alleviate the situation, attacks continued and the law was not consistently upheld.

Cable Street temporarily drew another 2,000 into the East London BUF, which used the March 1937 council elections to gauge its progress. Altogether, six fascist candidates stood in Bethnal Green, Shoreditch and Stepney, securing 20% of the total vote. But even in its East End 'heartland' the BUF could neither win seats nor markedly alter political allegiances. Subsequent election campaigns in London and the provinces all failed except in Suffolk, where the Eye district leader became a councillor in 1938.

Outbreak of war

These revival initiatives raised membership to an estimated 16,500 by December 1938 and the BUF's 'Stop the War' campaign of 1938–40 continued the upward trend. Mosley argued that peace and imperial security could be ensured by giving Germany a free hand in Eastern Europe and her former colonies (because British interests were unaffected) and by negotiating a disarmament pact between the four major West European nations. This policy blended principle with pragmatism. The blackshirts regarded many Nazi grievances as legitimate and genuinely wished to avoid entanglement in a European conflict. Mosley also realised that a war against the fascist powers would jeopardise the BUF's prospects. In July 1939, 20,000 attended the Earl's Court peace rally where Mosley reiterated his position and denounced 'Jewish schemes' to sour Anglo-German relations. By September 1939 membership had climbed to about 22,500.

During the 'phoney war', the BUF demanded a negotiated peace to preserve Britain and the Empire intact, but this was rejected at three parliamentary by-elections between February and May 1940. Popularly associated with Nazism, the organisation scraped 1–3% of the vote in these contests. The collapse of the Western Front in spring 1940 raised the spectre of invasion and induced unsubstantiated government fears that the BUF was a potential Nazi fifth column. Official concern concentrated on Mosley's tenuous connections with other key figures on the British fascist fringe in 1939–40, notably the Tory MP Archibald Ramsey, whose political secretary had allegedly passed sensitive material to the Germans. The authorities also wished to preserve public order by shielding the blackshirts from growing popular hostility. From May 1940, 747 British fascists, including Mosley, were interned under Defence Regulation 18(b) and in July the BUF was banned. The atmosphere of alarm and suspicion prompted the round-up of approximately 26,000 German, Austrian and Italian aliens as well.

Internal problems of the movement

Fascist propaganda depicted the BUF as a thriving, organised movement, united behind an infallible leader. The internal reality was quite different. Mosley was a poor tactician, an indifferent judge of character and was too credulous. Officials could ingratiate themselves by providing him with glowing progress reports which were frequently inaccurate. Partly because of these defects, Mosley's delegation of administrative and organisational functions tended to leave mediocrities and incompetents in charge.

Economic difficulties continually dogged the BUF. Under Robert Forgan, the first deputy leader, financial control barely existed and in the mid–1930s, widespread petty theft depleted BUF funds. The problem of financing the movement on a small paying membership became critical in the later 1930s when foreign aid was drying up. Drastic cuts slashed expenditure by 70% in 1937 alone and reduced the payroll from 350 to 50 between 1936 and 1939. As the central administration contracted under economic pressure, its ability to control the regions declined and increasingly local branches had to fend for themselves, despite the dedication of remaining officials and volunteers.

One of Mosley's prime objectives was to conceal the chief sources of fascist finance, particularly Italian funding. Between 1933 and 1936 Mussolini provided approximately £60,000 to keep the BUF afloat and, although British sympathisers also donated, only Mosley himself contributed more (about £100,000), mainly in the later 1930s. As Italian finance evaporated, from 1937 the BUF leader entered into covert negotiations for commercial radio franchises in Belgium, Ireland and Denmark and from the Dame of Sark. He had also secretly persuaded Hitler to provide a radio transmitter in Germany. The profits from such operations, which were never completed, were to be injected into the BUF.

These weaknesses were exacerbated by a basic division within the leadership between those who favoured a 'military' approach based on order, discipline and marches and a 'political' faction devoted to the dissemination of fascist propaganda. Mosley eventually concluded that the 'militarists' led by Francis Hawkins were more effective recruiters than the 'politicals' under William Joyce, John Beckett and A.K. Chesterton. In 1937, Mosley, fully accepting the militarist strategy, subjected Joyce's group to economic cuts. Joyce, Beckett and Chesterton all left the movement

Who were the fascists?

Information on the BUF's social base is sparse, but cautious generalisations can be made about the fluctuating membership. During the 1930s, fascist support shifted socially and geographically. As the organisation expanded until mid–1934, Mosley was able to forge a broad, mainly middle-class coalition which included ex-servicemen, disgruntled professionals, public school types, farmers, some small traders and disaffected Tories, unhappy with the government's Indian policy. These supporters tended to come from London (outside the East End), the south east, rural East Anglia, the Midlands and Yorkshire. The BUF also tapped the unemployed in Manchester and Liverpool.

After Olympia and the Rothermere interlude, membership shrank drastically and the various sectional campaigns placed the organisation on a more working-class footing. Textile and shipping policies attracted working-class northerners in Lancashire, Yorkshire and Liverpool for a time. Propaganda directed at small traders and businesses promising protection against larger competitors and 'proletarianisation' gained petty bourgeois adherents in northern England and the East End. Between 1935 and 1938 the BUF's attitude to Jewry rallied sizeable East London support from working-class, self-employed and petty bourgeois groups as well as from youths and anti-semites. Mosley's greatest political success came in this area which could boast over 2,000 activists and extensive latent support.

In 1938–39, numerous blackshirts in Bethnal Green, Limehouse and East Ham rejected the movement's pro-German line on patriotic grounds. However, this partial decline in the East End was more than offset by the BUF's peace campaign which attracted an older, more middle-class and right-wing following. Government intelligence indicated that fascist support in 1939–40 derived mainly from the upper and middle classes. The organisation became a sanctuary for many appeasers, dejected Conservatives and anti-war protesters, stimulating fresh growth in London (outside the East End) and across southern and eastern England.

Failure of British fascism

The failure of Mosley's fascist 'revolt' cannot be attributed merely to the shortcomings of the BUF or its leader. External factors played a major role in ensuring that British fascism never achieved any real prominence in the 1930s. Firstly, the party system, much maligned by Mosley, resolutely refused to collapse. From 1931, the Conservative-dominated National government provided a safe haven for the propertied classes and thereby denied the BUF political space on the right in which to develop as a credible alternative. Even after the trauma of 1931, the Labour Party was able to retain its traditional strongholds and much of its electoral support. Organised labour proved especially resistant to fascist appeals and

Mosley was unable to convert many of the unemployed. By and large, the jobless were not radicalised and could not be dislodged from their Labour and trade union allegiances, even in blackspots such as South Wales, central Scotland and north east England.

Secondly, as Mosley later admitted, the BUF had not been created early enough to take political advantage of the slump. Government measures such as the abandonment of the Gold Standard in 1931, low interest rates, limited reflation and empire preference after 1932, combined with an increase in real wages to help revive the economy. Between 1933 and 1937 Britain achieved 4% growth per annum, unemployment fell from 22.8% to 9.5% and output and real wages exceeded 1929 levels. BUF hopes of translating economic discontent into fascist support faded. The durability of the parliamentary system and the recovering economy also made Mosley's argument that fascism was needed to counter the communist 'threat' unconvincing.

In several respects, the BUF was alien to Britain's mainstream political culture. Its anti-democratic ethos and authoritarian programme were inimical to the liberal parliamentary tradition. The trappings of British fascism, such as the uniform and insignia, reminded the public of Hitler's and Mussolini's regimes and the excesses of the fascist states produced unfavourable domestic popular reactions to the BUF. In addition, Mosley's unwillingness to criticise either fascist leader raised public suspicions about the nature of his connections with the dictators. Since then, financial and commercial links have been uncovered. Finally, the movement's use of anti-semitism and its associated violence reaped rewards in the East End but further alienated the bulk of public opinion.

British fascism was contained too by the disruptive tactics of anti-fascist activists and state management. Opponents successfully saddled the BUF with the public blame for violence and disorder. The blackshirts were also placed under state surveillance from November 1933 and, after Rothermere and Mosley had parted company in July 1934, official pressure marginalised the BUF through a publicity boycott. Newspaper editors and the BBC were advised not to report fascist activities or publicise pro-Mosley views. At local level, the BUF also found it increasingly difficult to hire council property for meetings. Only when faced with public order problems, as in October 1936, or the invasion threat of 1940, did the State take more drastic action against Mosley and his followers.

Further reading

Cross, C. *The Fascists in Britain* (Barrie and Rockcliffe, 1961).

Cullen, S. 'The development of the ideas and policy of the British Union of Fascists, 1932–40', *Journal of Contemporary History*, Vol. 22 (1987).

Durham, M. 'Women and the British Union of Fascists, 1932–40', *Immigrants and Minorities*, Vol. 8 (1989).
Holmes, C. *Anti-semitism in British Society 1876–1939* (Arnold, 1979).
Lewis, D. *Illusions of Grandeur: Mosley, Fascism and British Society 1931–81* (Manchester University Press, 1987).
Lunn, K. and Thurlow, R. (eds) *British Fascism* (Croom Helm, 1980).
Mosley, O. *My Life* (Nelson, 1968).
Skidelsky, R. *Oswald Mosley* (Macmillan, 1975).
Thurlow, R. *Fascism in Britain: A History 1918–85* (Blackwell, 1987).
Webber, G. *The Ideology of the British Right 1918–39* (Croom Helm, 1986).

Andrew Mitchell lectures at Basingstoke College of Technology and is currently completing research on the BUF at Sheffield University.

Frank McDonough
Why Appeasement?

What were the motives and difficulties which led successive British governments to pursue a policy of appeasement?

The task of explaining why appeasement became the policy adopted by the British government to meet the unfolding European crisis of the 1930s is extremely difficult. There was no one single cause. The adoption of the policy by the British government was not inevitable – nor was appeasement the only policy on offer. To explain fully the reasons for appeasement it is necessary to take account of several factors.

Impact of war

The impact of the First World War was extremely important. The Great War was viewed as 'the war to end all wars' and in its aftermath the British public became disenchanted with the use of force in international relations. Anti-war books, films and poems all proved popular. A number of pacifist pressure groups – the Peace Pledge Union, the Peace Society and the No More War Movement – all compaigned for peaceful solutions to international problems. Thousands of war memorials were erected throughout Britain to mourn the dead of the First World War. Remembrance Sunday (11 November) became an annual day of mourning. There was a general feeling the war had been fought for no real social, economic or political gain. As a result, disarmament and peace became vote winners in elections. This widespread public mood infected the politicians and influenced the tone and conduct of British foreign policy.

Faith in the League of Nations

There was great idealistic faith among the British public for the League of Nations. A large proportion of the British public saw the League as preferable to armed force. It was set up at the Paris Peace Conference in 1919, with the aim of settling international disputes between nations by negotiation. The aim was for the League to act as arbitrator in disputes between nations and to provide collective security against military aggression. The League had the power to impose economic sanctions, threaten a potential aggressor with a collective attack by League members, and – as a last resort – remove an aggressor by military means. The burden of keeping peace in the world was to be shared by all nations. At its peak in 1931 the League of Nations Union had over 400,000 members. Yet it was too little appreciated by its supporters that the League could act as peace-keeper only so long as it enjoyed the full support of the majority of the world's great powers. By 1937, only Britain, France and Russia, of the major world powers, were still members.

Opposition to the Treaty of Versailles

There was a widespread feeling in Britain that the Treaty of Versailles had punished Germany too harshly for starting and losing the First World War. The main provisions of the treaty were:

- The German Army was to be limited to 100,000 and conscription banned.
- The German Navy was to be reduced to a coastal force and the building of submarines and battleships prohibited.
- A German Air Force was prohibited.
- Germany to lose European territory including Alsace-Lorraine, Eupen, Malmedy, North Schleswig, West Prussia, Poznania, parts of Upper Silesia and Memel.
- All Germany's non-European colonies to be placed under League of Nations control.
- Danzig to be made a 'free city' under League of Nations control.
- The Saar coalmining region was to be placed under League control until 1935.
- All foreign currency and gold to be confiscated.
- Union with Austria was forbidden.
- Germany was ordered to pay £6,600 million in reparations for war damage and pensions inflicted on Britain, Italy and France.
- Germany had to accept guilt for starting the war.
- Germany had to agree to accept a democratic constitution.

Source: Taylor. A.J.P. *The Origins of the Second World War* (Hamilton, 1961).

Public opinion

There was widespread public opposition in Britain to increased military expenditure. The collapse of the world economy not only made the atmosphere to rearm unfavourable; it also encouraged hostility to war. British public opinion as expressed in general elections, opinion polls, and by-elections revealed strong opposition towards re-armament. In a by-election at East Fulham in October 1933 a pacifist Labour candidate gained a seat from a Conservative candidate who campaigned for rearmament. In 1935 a nationwide public opinion poll organised by the Peace Pledge Union showed how unpopular rearmament was with the British public.

The imperial dimension

The 'white dominions' of the British Empire (Canada, Australia, South Africa, New Zealand,) all strongly opposed supporting Britain in a second world war. The growing nationalist movements in India, Egypt, Iraq and Palestine were more concerned to gain independence than to fight for British interests. Yet in the hostile economic climate of the 1930s trade with the empire was even more vital to the British economy than ever before. There was a widespread view in British government circles that if Britain went to war again in Europe it would risk breaking up the empire.

The weakness of British armed forces

The poor state of Britain's armed forces greatly influenced the adoption of the policy of appeasement. Britain remained a large naval power, but the army and airforce were in a very poor condition. In 1933 Britain was in no position to defend the country from air attack, let alone defend France and its empire. It is worth looking more closely at the state of British defences during the 1930s:

(a) The Navy

The key to British security from invasion was the Royal Navy. This was greatly reduced in strength from the pre-1914 period but still remained more powerful than all but the American fleet (Table 1).

The Admiralty constantly advised the British government to ensure that British foreign policy was arranged to avoid a war breaking out against Germany, Italy and Japan simultaneously.

	Battleships	Aircraft Carriers	Submarines
Great Britain	15	6	57
Germany	5	0	65
France	7	1	78
Italy	4	0	104
Japan	9	5	60
USSR	3	0	18
USA	15	5	57

Table 1: Naval Strength of the Great Powers (1939)[1]

They warned that such an eventuality would severely weaken the ability of the Navy to defend merchant shipping from attack and enforce an effective blockade against the enemy.

(b) The Army

The role of the army had always been a secondary consideration in British policy. Conscription in peacetime was viewed as beyond the pale of British life. The only time Britain had maintained a substantial army was during the First World War, when 70 divisions were created. At the end of the First World War the army was greatly reduced. In relation to the German army of Adolf Hitler the British army was a David in the face of a Goliath (Table 2 and 3).

Home Defence	107,000
British India and Burma army	55,000
Indian army	190,000
Middle East	21,000
Far East	12,000
West Indies	2,000
Total	387,000

Table 2: Size and Distribution of British Army (1938)[2]

Home Defence	730,000
Trained Conscripts	2,970,000

Table 3: The Size of the German Army (1939)[3]

In full knowledge of these figures, the British Generals urged the government to pursue a policy of peaceful negotiation. The idea of sending a great army to France was abandoned. The Chiefs of Staff based their strategy on the principle of 'limited liability'. This meant Britain was only committed to sending a maximum of four army divisions to France in the event of a war with Germany. This strategy weakened the position of France *vis à vis* Germany and Italy (Table 4).

(c) The Air Force

The Royal Air Force was the newest of the three services. In the 1920s it was given the lowest priority of all three services. Yet as the German threat became more menacing, it rose to become the

	January 1938	August 1939
Germany	81	130
Italy	73	73
France	63	86
USSR	125	125
Czechoslovakia	34	0
Poland	40	40
Great Britain	2	41

Table 4: Army Divisions committed to European war[4]

Note: This was the size of force immediately available in September 1939, although Britain was committed to sending a further 39 divisions when they had completed military training.

	1932	1933	1934	1935	1936	1937	1938	1939
France	600	600	600	785	890	743	1,382	3,163
Great Britan	445	633	740	1,140	1,877	2,153	2,827	7,941
Germany	36	368	1,968	3,183	5,112	5,606	5,235	8,295
Italy	500	500	750	1,000	1,500	1,500	1,850	0000

Table 5: Aircraft Production of the Great Powers (1932–39)[5]

highest priority in British national defence. The reason was the fear of the damage air bombing could inflict on the civilian population. It became widely recognised that in a future war British cities ran the risk of being bombed to the ground. This fear grew as the tension mounted. By 1938 expenditure on the RAF was even higher than the Royal Navy or the army. Table 5 shows the growth of the RAF in relation to the other major World powers.

In 1935 a secret report commissioned by the National government on the condition and requirements of Britain's armed forces revealed a navy no longer able to defend Europe and the empire, an army so small and poorly equipped in tanks and artillery it could offer little help to France in the event of a German assault and an air force with few long-range bombers, few fighter plans and no adequate aircraft defence. The report blamed faith in the League of Nations and the general public mood against rearmament for the poor state of Britain's defences. The report concluded that Britain was not only incapable of defeating Germany, Japan and Italy and defending the empire in any future conflagration: Britain was not even capable of adequately defending *British* cities from air attack. The government was urged to increase public expenditure on the armed services, improve air defence and direct foreign policy to avoid fighting a war against Japan, Germany and Italy simultaneously.

The Treasury opposed rearmament

The Treasury consistently opposed greatly increased expenditure on rearmament. Neville Chamberlain, Chancellor of the Exchequer 1931–37, was the most consistent supporter of this view before he became Prime Minister. He consistently argued as Chancellor of the Exchequer that rearmament would damage the fragile recovery of the economy from the 'great depression' by diverting skilled workers away from the peacetime economy. The Treasury believed the defence industry could only be expanded at the expense of reductions in public expenditure on health and pensions, the improvement of which had been a major concern of Chamberlain as Minister

	Defence	Health and National Insurance	Pensions
1919	692	74	100
1920	292	73	110
1921	189	73	96
1922	111	61	83
1923	105	59	72
1924	114	65	71
1925	119	65	70
1926	116	75	65
1927	117	73	62
1928	113	76	59
1929	113	86	56
1930	110	108	55
1931	107	121	52
1932	103	155	49
1933	107	151	49
1934	113	151	47
1935	136	162	46
1936	186	162	45
1937	197	162	44
1938	254	166	43

Table 6: Government Expenditure on Defence, Health and Pensions 1919–39 (in millions £)[6]

	Great Britain	Germany
1935	3.3	7.4
1936	4.2	12.4
1937	5.6	11.8
1938	8.1	16.6
1939	21.4	23.0
1940	51.7	38.0

Table 7: Percentage of Gross National Product devoted to Defence[7]

of Health in the 1920s. This meant rearmament could only be financed out of government borrowing which would push up inflation and possibly increase unemployment – which by 1937 was falling. Table 6 gives an indication of the spending priorities of the British government in the inter-war period.

Yet as the European crisis intensified in 1938 and 1939 even the Treasury began to change its view. As Table 6 shows, the period when the German threat was at its height, saw the most spectacular rise in defence expenditure. Table 7 shows what percentage of its overall industrial production Britain was devoting to defence, in comparison with Nazi Germany.

By 1940 Britain was devoting a higher proportion of the GNP to defence than even Germany.

Conclusion

Appeasement grew out of an intermingling of all these factors. It was against this complex backround that the British government adopted the policy of appeasement. This is not to say appeasement was inevitable, or the only logical solution to the reality of the international situation in the late 1930s. It is merely to give due emphasis to the difficult circumstances and choices available to the British government in formulating and executing its foreign and defence policy. In the context of the times appeasement was a logical and a sensible policy for the British government to follow. This was how it seemed to Neville Chamberlain when he came to power in 1937. It fitted the general public mood which had developed in British society in the aftermath of the First World War. The policy of appeasement offered to Neville Chamberlain an historic opportunity – as he saw it – to solve German grievances by peaceful negotiation and save Europe from further death and destruction in a second world war.

Notes

(1) Adamthwaite, A. *The Making of the Second World War* (Allen and Unwin, 1977).
(2) Bell, P.M.H. *The Origins of The Second World War in Europe* (Longman, 1986).
(3) Bell, P.M.H. *The Origins of the Second World War in Europe* (Longman, 1986).
(4) Adamthwaite, A. *The Making of the Second World War* (Allen and Unwin, 1977).
(5) Kennedy, P. *The Rise and Fall of the Great Powers* (Unwin Hyman, 1988).
(6) Butler, D. and Butler, (ed) G. *British Political Facts* (Macmillan, 1986).
(7) Peden, G.C. 'A Matter of Timing: The Economic Background to British Foreign Policy 1937–39' (*Historical Journal, 1983*).

Frank McDonough lectures in Modern Political History at Liverpool John Moores University.

Peter Catterall

Labour and Appeasement

Peter Catterall examines the other side of appeasement by looking at the extent to which the Labour opposition offered a viable alternative to the National government's strategy.

The questions of how peace can be maintained, international aggression met and under what circumstances, if any, war is justifiable, were perennial problems for our compatriots in the inter-war years. The answers the National government gave to these problems have received extensive scrutiny over the ensuing years. One of the first books to examine this policy was that by 'Cato' (Michael Foot and others) entitled *Guilty Men*. That the National government had ultimately failed in its efforts to maintain peace was certainly clear. But in what W.H. Auden described in his poem '1st September 1939' as the 'low, dishonest decade' of the 1930s, who had answered the tortuous moral questions posed by the diplomacy of the period correctly and did they include the Labour Party to which Foot belonged?

The Labour Party was in opposition from August 1931 until the formation of the wartime coalition in May 1940. This long period of opposition explains why the party's attitudes to the diplomatic problems of the period have attracted relatively little attention. However, it is about time that the extent to which the Labour Party was offering a coherent alternative to the National government's approach to these problems, in its role as the official opposition, was properly scrutinised.

The response to the First World War

The party's attitude to the maintenance of peace was founded upon its response to the outbreak of the First World War. Some in the party opposed the war either on moral grounds or because, in their view, it was a capitalist and imperial war. Most of the party, however, supported the war, defending their stance on the basis of a Christian duty to protect small nations. Their views on how to prevent a similar conflagration occurring again, a major preoccupation of many politicians throughout the inter-war period, were meanwhile being informed by the views of the Union of Democratic Control (UDC) formed in 1914. The policies developed by this body were derived from its criticism of the policies and the international system which had failed to prevent conflict in 1914. In December 1917 virtually the whole programme of the UDC – complete democratisation of all countries; the limitation of armaments; the abolition of private arms manufacture; the establishment of an international court and legislature; self-determination and the holding of plebiscites to decide territorial disputes – was endorsed at a special Labour Party conference.

Such recommendations reflected and informed the faith of the time in a restructured international system as a guarantor of peace. This system, as it emerged from the chaos of war at the summit meetings at Versailles, was a grave disappointment, however, to the architects of these recommendations.

Labour nevertheless accepted the value of the principal creation of Versailles – the League of Nations. Its 1928 programme, *Labour and the Nation*, spoke of renunciation of war, to be replaced by negotiation through the League of Nations, an objective which Ramsay MacDonald strove hard to further during the short Labour government of 1924. When Labour took office for the second time in 1929 its foreign policy priorities remained very much the same as those defined by the UDC.

The assumption on which these rested – that all international conflict is susceptible of peaceful, rational solution – provided a broad area of consensus between pacifists and non-pacifists within the party. Limited progress towards naval disarmament through the negotiations that culminated in the 1930 London naval treaty perhaps went some way towards justifying these assumptions. In 1930 it was announced that no more capital ships would be build until 1936. In the same year the withdrawal of the last Allied troops from the Rhineland marked a further stage in the return of Germany to the concert of nations. Plans were meanwhile laid for the resolution of international differences at the Geneva disarmament conference starting in 1932, to be chaired by the Labour Foreign Secretary, Arthur Henderson.

The gathering storm

The conference, however, did not develop into a triumphal display of the virtues of UDC ideals. The total failure of the conference, after Germany had deserted it for the second and final time in October 1933, together with the simultaneous rise of the sinister and unscrupulous figure of Hitler, increasingly called into question the assumptions on which Labour's defence and foreign policy had been based.

In 1929 disarmament had been seen both as a way of reducing international tension and supplying a moral lead. In the wake of the Japanese attack on Manchuria, such assumptions became increasingly difficult to sustain.

There was, however, a reluctance to abandon long-held attitudes. Indeed, the 1933 party conference responded to the worsening international situation by returning to the pre–1914 policy of calling a general strike in the event of war. The muzzling of trade unions in Fascist countries made this policy futile and it was dropped the following year. But an emphasis on rational negotiation and international arms control remained much in evidence. At the same time, there was a growing awareness that if this failed, collective action might be necessary to curb an aggressor state. In 1934 the party therefore recommended a 'Yes' vote to every question in the League of Nations Union Peace Ballot, including one approving of military action against an aggressor.

The following year the need to react to Mussolini's invasion of Abyssinia made the implications of this, for the TUC at least, extremely clear. Its Secretary, Walter Citrine, told Congress that 'there is only one way to deal with a bully and that is by the use of force'. The TUC overwhelmingly agreed.

Those in the party opposed to all war had supported Labour's pacific but non-pacifist policy in the 1920s, but they could not accept such a policy. They became increasingly isolated. At the 1935 party conference, debating the same resolution calling for sanctions against Italy which the TUC had so heavily endorsed, the trade union leader, Ernest Bevin, launched a furious attack on the compromises the pacifist George Lansbury had been led into through his position as party leader, prompting his resignation shortly thereafter. From 1936 pacifists made little impact on party conferences. They were not, however, without importance in the 1930s. Baldwin later attributed to the triumph of the Labour candidate John Wilmot, standing on a pacifist platform in the 1933 East Fulham by-election, the government's reluctance to begin its rearmament programme earlier.

Pacifists in the party meanwhile retained their faith in international arbitration as the solution of the economic and territorial tensions they saw as leading to war. Even after war broke out, in November 1939 a group of MPs put their names to a memorandum calling for an immediate armistice and a conference of this type.

Labour and the preparation for war

Even those who had abandoned faith in such solutions were reluctant to be seen doing anything to prepare for war. The Air Raid Precautions introduced in 1935 were widely criticised as likely to produce a war atmosphere, despite a party circular declaring that they were necessary.The Service Estimates, in which Parliament voted money for the armed forces, were opposed until 1936 (thereafter Labour abstained). The 1937 Defence Loans Bill, designed to increase spending on rearmament, received the same treatment.

At the same time there was a growing sense of frustration with the inadequacy of the government's diplomacy and its civil defence preparations. This was confirmed by the 1938 Munich crisis. The threat to Czechoslovakia that prompted it was a casus belli for Labour. But the reluctance actually to prepare for war persisted. The limited degree of conscription hastily introduced after Hitler's invasion of Czechoslovakia in Spring 1939 was again opposed by Labour. In retrospect it seemed to Morgan Phillips Price:

> We wanted to stand up to Hitler and Mussolini, but thought it should only be done through the League of Nations. Labour opinion was confused. We were afraid to re-arm in the ordinary way because we had argued ourselves into thinking that all armament meant war. We could not bring ourselves to believe that they might deter an aggressor.

Whether Labour would have been a more formidable opponent for the dictators remains in doubt. Certainly after the war broke out it remained resolute: after Dunkirk, as Halifax and Chamberlain contemplated mediation, the Labour members of the War Cabinet supported Churchill's defiance. Before September 1939 it had done much to create the mood in favour of peace and international arbitration which formed the backdrop to appeasement. In the vital years of the 1930s its policy can be contrasted with that of the National government in that it was both less willing to appease the dictators *and* to prepare for war against them. Once its UDC certainties were thrust aside by circumstances, its policies were indeed confused, and it is against this yardstick that the National government's appeasement should be measured. If the National government was guilty, then it seems unlikely that the incoherent opposition Labour offered should be totally absolved. In both cases, however, 'guilt', such as it is, consists in pursuing the best of intentions – the maintenance of peace. Moral judgements should not be used to damn the ultimately unsuccessful efforts of governments and parties to solve the colossal diplomatic problems of the period. Foot, if he was a Christian, would know better than to cast the first stone.

Peter Catterall is Executive Director of the Institute of Contemporary British History and visiting Lecturer in History at Queen Mary and Westfield College, London.

PART III
War and Welfare

Britain had ended the First World War with a larger empire than ever, thanks to the addition of League of Nations mandate territories such as Tanganyika and Palestine. These far-flung responsibilities had to be defended with slender resources. Allocating the necessary finance diverted resources from other projects. 'What a fearful bill do we owe to Master Hitler', Neville Chamberlain accordingly complained in 1937.

The problem of resource allocation worsened after the Second World War. Money had somehow to be found from a limited budget to meet the pressing needs for civil and industrial reconstruction. At the same time the international situation deteriorated much more rapidly than had been anticipated. By 1947 the Labour government felt constrained to introduce peacetime conscription for the first time in Britain in order to meet its commitments.

After the First World War it had been possible to introduce a ten year rule, during which no serious conflict was envisaged. The Attlee government was denied such a luxury. The first signs of the Cold War were indeed already upon it. It inherited from the wartime Coalition involvement in the Greek Civil War against the Communists, and embroilment in action to restore French and Dutch control in Vietnam and Indonesia respectively against Communist guerrillas. By 1948 the British were also combatting Communist guerrillas in their own territories in Malaya. At the same time Britain was the main guaranteeing power in that strategically most important area, the oil-rich Middle East, as well as being the main Western military power in Europe. This range of commitments reflected not so much the desire to maintain the illusion of great power status as the continuation of great power responsibilities.

Some commitments nevertheless had to go. There was a painful withdrawal from the intercommunal conflict that had made Palestine impossible by 1948. In India, in contrast, the inability of nationalist politicians to control intercommunal violence led to a greater willingness to meet British hopes that India, after independence in 1947, would remain inside the Sterling Area and the Commonwealth. The same year saw the Americans effectively replace the British in Greece.

Involving the Americans in this way was the preferred means of dealing with the constraints on Britain. American assistance was crucial in resolving economic as well as security problems. In 1946 Keynes negotiated an American loan to stabilise Britain's finances. It failed to do so, and by the following year Britain needed further assistance. Growing American appreciation of British and European economic problems was marked early in 1948 by agreement to merge the British and American occupation zones in Germany for economic purposes; a development which was soon followed by Marshall Aid to support European economic recovery, administered through the British-led Organisation for European Economic Co-operation. At the same time the Soviet threat led first Britain and then America to make unprecedented commitments to the security of Western Europe, culminating in the formation of the North Atlantic Treaty Organisation in April 1949.

Although this marked a military commitment, followed by the creation of the British Army of the Rhine after 1954, there was little enthusiasm for closer European economic and political unity. The empire remained important economically as well as psychologically. It was only with the shift in trade towards a revived Europe in the 1950s that the idea that Britain's economic future lay there began to gain widespread currency amongst politicans and businessmen.

Martin Gilbert
Winston Churchill

Churchill is best remembered as Prime Minister of wartime Britain. But, as Martin Gilbert his official biographer shows, this was by no means his only contribution to recent British history.

Winston Churchill is best known for his leadership during the Second World War, when he was Prime Minister at the head of an all-party coalition. During more than five years, from May 1940 to July 1945, he was the vocal and active head of a nation determined not to give in to the threats posed by Germain air raids, and which, after much of Europe had been overrun by the German forces, was equally determined not to give up the struggle to survive, and in due course to participate fully in the defeat of Nazi Germany. Churchill's speeches as war leader inspired a sense of national purpose. As the head of the War Cabinet, he encouraged his ministers, his chiefs of staff, and the civil servants to persevere when times were grim, and to plan ahead for the eventual landings in Northern Europe and the military assault on the territory of Germany.

When he became Prime Minister in May 1940 Churchill was 65 years old. Behind him were 40 years of intense political activity and experience of public life and administration. He had entered Parliament as a 24 year old Conservative in 1900, after a dramatic and much-publicised escape from a Boer prisoner-of-war-camp in South Africa had made him, overnight, a well-known figure throughout Britain. From his first months in Parliament he had shown that he would not accept party discipline uncritically, and was quick at criticising party policy where he felt that it was cynical or inhumane. He opposed the imposition of British rule by force on the people of Tibet, telling a Conservative colleague: 'Surely it is very wicked to do such things. Absolute contempt for the rights of others must be wrong.'

This was to be a consistent theme. In the House of Commons in 1920, when he was Secretary of State for War, he defended the government for having censured a British general who had opened fire at Amritsar on a large number of unarmed Indians, and told the House of Commons that the shooting was 'a monstrous event'. If the British Empire could not exist on the basis of armed force, he argued, then it had no moral basis. He was convinced that British rule could be humane and beneficial: for this reason he wished to see it continued in India. But when Indian autonomy was put on the statute book in 1935, he at once sent a message to the Indian leader, M.K. Gandhi: 'I do not care if you are more or less loyal to Britain, what matters is the lot of the Indian people. Use the powers that are offered and make the thing a success.'

Churchill's disaffection with rigid Conservatism had led him, in 1904, to join the Liberal Party, then in opposition. For more than a year he was a leading figure in the political battles that led to the triumph of the Liberals at the general election and their formation of a government. From the first days of that government he was given ministerial responsibility. He relished hard work, and sought to establish broad principles of administration. His energies led him to be asked to devise a constitution for the recently defeated Boer republics. He did so, seeking to eliminate vindictiveness from the settlement, and urging an end to the animosities of formerly bitter foes.

Legislation

As a Liberal Minister, Churchill put on the statute book several important pieces of legislation to improve the lot of the working man and woman. His Labour Exchanges Act sets up centres where the unemployed could learn about the availability of jobs. His Shops Act made meal breaks at work compulsory. He advocated the nationalisation of the railways, and devised the basic scheme for State-aided unemployment and sickness insurance. He sought arbitration rather than confrontation in industrial disputes: to this end he established in 1908 a Standing Court of Arbitration. His aim was to find a middle way between capitalism and socialism: in a public speech in 1906 he explained:

> I do not want to see impaired the vigour of competition, but we can do much to mitigate the consequences of failure. We want to draw a line below which we will not allow persons to live and labour.

As Home Secretary in 1910, Churchill turned his reforming zeal to prison reform. The common punishment of solitary confinement was drastically reduced, as was the age at which young people could be imprisoned. The number of youths sent to Borstal was reduced. Imprisonment for non-payment of fines was replaced by the principle of 'time to pay'. In explaining his philosophy of punishment to the House of Commons, he advocated 'a calm and dispassionate recognition of the rights of the accused against the State, and even of convicted criminals against the State'. Churchill always believed that the State had an obligation to involve itself in the improvement of the life of the citizen, especially the disadvantaged citizen. To this end, shortly after he became Chancellor of the Exchequer in 1924, and returned to the Conservative Party which he had left 20 years earlier, he introduced State-aided widows and orphans pensions.

On the political platform, Churchill was a brilliant, outspoken, witty and often savage critic of those against whom he fought. During the first general election of 1910, when he advocated a drastic reduction in the power of the House of Lords, he was pitiless in his attacks. This made him many life-long enemies, particularly among the Conservatives whose ranks he had abandoned in 1904, and against whose policies he had turned with relentless public criticisms. When he attacked those judges whose verdicts were, in his view, too harsh in cases against trade unions, and too severe in the cases of young offenders, he was again denounced by the Conservatives. When he insisted, during riots in the Welsh mining village of Tonypandy, that troops who had been sent for from London be ordered off the train, and London policemen sent in their place, he was again criticised by the Conservative newspapers for undue leniency. In his defence, Churchill told the House of Commons: 'It must be an object of public policy to avoid collisions between troops and people engaged in industrial disputes.'

Conciliation

Churchill's instinct in both domestic and international crises was always for conciliation. At the height of the constitutional struggle over the House of Lords in 1910, he proposed a compromise between the ruling Liberals and opposition Conservatives based upon recognition of Conservative fears. In 1914 he sought a formula whereby Britain and Germany could resolve their naval rivalry without war. Successive Prime Ministers called upon him to try to devise formulas in areas of long-standing controversy. It was Churchill who negotiated the settlement with the Irish nationalists in 1921 which led to the setting up of the Irish Free State. Likewise, following the short but bitter General Strike in 1926, he sought to devise a system whereby the grievances of the miners could be met, and the owners forced to make concessions.

In foreign affairs, through his 55 years in public life, Churchill was likewise the advocate of compromise. After the First World War, he urged the government not to pursue a vindictive policy against the defeated Germans, but to bring Germany into the European security system. After the Second World War, he urged Germany's presence in the Council of Europe, and participation in any European defence system. He had faith that the democratic States, if they were willing to act together, could deter the aggression of dictators, and thus avoid war. He called the Second World War 'the Unnecessary War', believing that if the European democracies had stood together, and if Britain had supported their efforts, Hitler would not have had the strength to attack them, and, as happened, to destroy them one by one.

Tyranny excited Churchill's deepest dislike. He was a leading advocate of Western support for those Russians who, in 1918 and 1919, sought to curb and to destroy the new Bolshevik regime. He was angry when the Prime Minister, David Lloyd George, decided to withdraw that support, and made Churchill himself responsible for the withdrawal of all British troops from Russia. Nazism likewise seemed to him to be a creed with which there could be no compromise. In 1933 he was one of the first Members of Parliament to denounce the racist and militaristic aspects of the Nazi creed. In a speech in Paris in 1936, he urged his listeners to avoid both extremes, and to stand instead by the democratic ideals which gave mankind their greatest hope of fair play and justice.

In his four-volume work, *A History of the English-speaking Peoples*, written on the eve of the Second World War, Churchill sought to explain the evolution of democratic institutions and the importance of maintaining them. Within a month of the German occupation of Prague in 1939, he wrote to one of his literary assistants on the book:

> In the main, the theme is emerging of the growth of freedom and law, of the rights of the individual, of the subordination of the State to the fundamental and moral conceptions of an ever-comprehending community. Of these ideas the English-speaking peoples were the authors, then the trustees, and must now become the armed champions. Thus I condemn tyranny in whatever guise and from whatever quarter it presents itself.

War

Despite his firmly-held belief that war could have been avoided, and ought to have been avoided both in 1914 and 1939, by foresight, and by resolute government initiative, Churchill's main contribution to British national life was in time of war. In the First World War, as First Lord of the Admiralty, he devised several military schemes including the unsuccessful attack on Turkey at the Dardanelles. In 1917 Lloyd George made him Minister of Munitions, charged with the mass manufacture of weapons of war. He was a pioneer in the development of the tank, and in the evolution of airpower. In 1939 he was brought back to the Admiralty, where he again devised many plans for action, including the dropping of mines into the River Rhine, and the mining of neutral Norwegian territorial waters in an attempt to prevent German war supplies, obtained in Sweden, from reaching Germany by sea. As Prime Minister from 1940 to 1945 he was fertile in proposals to take the military initiative, to devise methods to avert defeat, and to find the most effective means of defeating Germany, Italy and Japan.

Yet Churchill was far from a warmonger. As a young man he had fought in three wars, in India, in the Sudan and in South Africa, and had relished the challenge of danger and leadership. The strategic challenges of war intrigued him, its situations of courage filled him with pride in the achievements of British soldiers. But he had seen the face of war close up, and from the turn of the century, including in his first speech in Parliament in 1901, he warned of the true nature of war, and of the terrible consequences of unleashing it. He wrote in a newspaper article during the Boer War in South Africa:

> Ah, horrible war, amazing medley of the glorious and the squalid, the pitiful and the sublime, if modern men of light and leading saw your face closer, simple folk would see it hardly ever.

In 1909, while an observer at German Army manoeuvres, he wrote to his wife:

> Much as war attracts me and fascinates my mind with its tremendous situations, I feel more deeply every year, and can measure the feeling here in the midst of arms, what vile and wicked folly and barbarism it all is.

At the height of the Second World War, on being shown a film of the bombing of a German city, he asked the man sitting next to him: 'Are we beasts? Are we taking this too far?'

And peace

After the Second World War, Churchill urged the unity of the West against the threat of Communist expansion, and warned the democracies that if they allowed themselves to be weak and divided, as they had been before the war, they would easily succumb to Soviet Russian ambitions. But at the same time, he expressed the view that the existence of nuclear bombs meant that any war would mean the destruction of mankind, and that the supreme need was for the reconciliation of conflicting ideologies. To this end he proposed that the leaders of the divided world meet and seek some common ground: the word he coined for such a meeting was 'summit'. After the death of Stalin in 1953, he urged his colleagues in the British Cabinet, and also the United States leaders, to try to set up such a summit with the new Soviet rulers. Much of his second Premiership, from 1951 to 1955, was devoted to seeking such a sumit, but neither his own Cabinet nor the American leaders, were keen. At the same time, he sought to limit the spread of the Korean and Indo-China wars, and declined an American request that Britain become involved in Vietnam.

Churchill was an extremely well-educated man, and himself the author of many books, including multi-volume histories of both world wars, and substantial biographies of his ancestor, John Churchill, the 1st Duke of Marlborough, and of his father, Lord Randolph Churchill. But he had no university education, his father having insisted that he go into the army. At school he excelled in many subjects, including English and history, though in a charming book of memoirs, *My Early Life*, written when he was in his mid-fifties, he pretended that he had been something of a dunce. In fact, he was a diligent schoolboy, was widely read, enjoyed every aspect of English, and was deeply-versed in the poetry, historical writing and general literature of his time.

At a time when his political fortunes were at a low ebb, after the failure at the Dardanelles in 1915, Churchill was persuaded to take up oil painting to distract his mind from the political blows. He did so, becoming an enthusiastic and prolific amateur painter, and often finding solace and solitude in painting at home and abroad. He was a lover of the English countryside, and from 1924 lived as often as he could at Chartwell, his country house in Kent, where he took great pleasure in every aspect of country life: redesigning the house itself, excavating lakes and building a swimming pool, supervising considerable farming activities, building walls with his own hands, and painting. At Chartwell he received many political visitors, was brought secret information about German rearmament in the 1930s, entertained lavishly, and enjoyed the company of his family.

Character and method

Churchill's circle of friends was a wide one. His company was always exhilarating, his conversation a fascinating blend of past memories and current affairs. His wit was legendary, his generosity considerable. A hard taskmaster whose subordinates and secretaries were expected to work long hours, he was at the same time generous in his praise and great fun to work with. Much of this work centred upon the preparation of speeches. Churchill wrote or dictated every word of the thousands of speeches that he made, then practised them on friends, sought the opinions of colleagues and of his wife Clementine, re-wrote and polished then, and virtually learned them by heart before delivering them.

A one-hour-speech often involved Churchill in two or three days preparation. He could hold a vast public audience in thrall, could hold the attention of the House of Commons for well over an hour, and could set out, in clear and often graphic language complex arguments and detailed proposals. His ability to pilot a bill through the House of Commons was much appreciated by the five Prime Ministers under whom he worked at different times, each of whom also turned to him to explain in public complicated or controversial issues. He never flinched in his speeches from giving bad news, or from putting forward politically unpopular views. In the 1930s this meant a constant opposition to the appeasement policies of Stanley Baldwin and Neville Chamberlain.

In the course of setting out his reasons for wanting greater rearmament and collective security, in order to deter Hitler from aggression, Churchill won the enmity of the political establishment, but the support of a wider and wider public, until, in the summer of 1939, the call for his return to the Cabinet reached the force of a national campaign. Following his return to the Cabinet in September 1939, and his elevation to the Premiership in May 1940, his speeches, including several broadcast ones, revived the national mood which had fallen into despondency.

As the German bombing of Britain intensified, and the sinking of merchant ships mounted, cutting Britain off from vital food supplies, Churchill's reiterated confidence in the justice of the Allied cause and his faith in ultimate victory were themselves a factor in maintaining the morale and enhancing the war-making capacity of the British people. In the lands occupied by Germany and tyrannised by the Gestapo, his words of defiance and confidence brought comfort to many whose lives were particularly wretched and endangered.

Churchill's commitment to democracy was total. He believed that the parliamentary system contained the greatest safeguards for the rights of the individual. For more than 60 years he was a member of the House of Commons, willing always to accept the verdict of the electorate, and to provide in opposition the same leadership and inventiveness as when he was in government. He was equally at home, and equally vigilant, in piloting bills through the House of Commons, and in opposing those bills with which he disagreed. He was a staunch upholder of the independence of the judiciary, and of the obligation of the State towards its citizens, whatever their status in society.

Churchill's belief in his own abilities was total. In 1916, when he was nearly killed in the trenches on the Western Front, he wrote to his wife of 'a loss to the war-making power of Britain that no one would ever know or measure or mourn.' History enabled those powers to become known, and to be exercised when most needed, between 1940 and 1945. But they were powers that he exercised in peace as well as in war, and which, across five decades, made their contribution to the safety and quality of British life.

Martin Gilbert is a Fellow of Merton College Oxford, and the author of six volumes of the biography of Winston Churchill, with supporting volumes of documents, as well as the single volume *Churchill: A Life* (Minerva, 1992).

Paul Addison
A New Jerusalem?

Recent work has reassessed the extent to which social policy in Britian was transformed during and after the Second World War.

Between 1940 and 1951 the social services in Britain were expanded and reorganised into 'the Welfare State'. But what was the Welfare State? The phrase itself only came into general use at the end of the 1940s, after the welfare reforms of the period were established. It implied a state which provided for all citizens a basic level of income and services through the social security system, the health service, housing, education, and the maintenance of full employment. More broadly, exponents of the Welfare State regarded it as the expression of a new social order based on the values of equality and community.

Continuity or change?

The Welfare State was long viewed by historians as one of the great radical achievements of a radical decade. But in recent years, the significance of welfare reforms has increasingly been called into question. Historians are more likely to emphasise the limitations of reform: the continuity with earlier policies, the failure to resolve problems, the persistence of social divisions. From the radical right an alternative critique has emerged, and the Welfare State is singled out as the prime cause of Britain's post-war economic decline. Before turning to these arguments, let us remind ourselves of the more salient developments in social policy between 1940 and 1951.

On the eve of the Second World War Britain was one of the most advanced of all countries in social provision. The majority of manual workers (but not their wives and children) were covered by compulsory social insurance schemes. The long-term unemployed, who had exhausted their entitlement to benefit, were eligible for means-tested relief from the Unemployment Assistance Board. The social services were complex and growing. State elementary schools and municipal hospitals were familiar landmarks. Ante-natal clinics and infant welfare centres were multiplying, and three million children received free or subsidised milk in school.

The social services were a patchwork without an overall design, but running through them were two connecting threads. Firstly, the social services were based on the principle of selectivity: they were intended for the lower income groups. The middle classes were expected to pay their doctor's bills, invest for old age, and bear the cost of their children's education. Secondly, it was assumed that self-help and voluntary action still had a large part to play. Welfare benefits were not intended to provide an income sufficient for a family to live on, and social services were still in part provided by charitable organisations like the voluntary hospitals.

The Beveridge Report

The first consequence of the outbreak of war in 1939 was the disruption of social services. But as the war intensified, parties and pressure groups advanced a multitude of plans for 'social reconstruction'. Of these the most important was the Beveridge Report of December 1942. William Beveridge was an eminent academic and civil servant whose ambition was to direct manpower policy. But he was much disliked by the Minister of Labour, Ernest Bevin, who sidetracked him into the chairmanship of an apparently insignificant committee on the future of social insurance. Beveridge turned his committee into the vehicle for an ambitious programme of social reform.

The principal aim of the Report was the abolition of 'Want' – poverty as defined by pre-war social surveys. Beveridge proposed a unified and comprehensive scheme of social insurance that would guarantee the income necessary for subsistence in the event of sickness, unemployment, and all other interruptions of income. The pre-war principle of selectivity was rejected in favour of universalism: the whole adult population was to be included, with a special policy for housewives. Beveridge also argued that his social insurance plan could only succeed as part of a comprehensive social policy which included family allowances, a national health service, and the prevention of mass unemployment. Want, he added with a flourish, was only one of five Giants on the road to reconstruction: the others were Disease, Ignorance, Squalor and Idleness.

Response to Beveridge

By chance the report appeared soon after the victory of the Eighth Army at El Alamein, a psychological turning-point between war and peace. It was acclaimed by most of the press, and the great majority of the public, as a plan that would prevent the poverty and mass unemployment which had followed the First World War. The response of the coalition government led by Winston Churchill was more complex. Conservative ministers recognised that the report was too popular to reject. Labour ministers recognised that it could not be adopted without thorough consideration. So the government responded by studying the report and producing its own proposals.

On the question of social security, ministers accepted Beveridge's plan for a unified and universal scheme, but rejected the principle of subsistence as unworkable. In the field of health, they committed themselves to the creation of a comprehensive National Health Service free at the point of treatment. In the case of family allowances the government again rejected the principle of subsistence, and scaled down the benefit. But the Family Allowances Act of 1945, a coalition measure, introduced a child allowance of five shillings per week for the second and all subsequent children, irrespective of means.

Strictly speaking it may seem that employment was a matter of economic rather than social policy. But the social reformers of the war years invariably included the abolition of mass unemployment as one of the indispensable elements of social reconstruction. This was partly due to the influence of the economist, John Maynard Keynes, whose *General Theory* had been published in 1936. Keynes argued that governments had the power to counteract a slump by raising the level of aggregate demand in the economy. The Coalition government's White Paper on employment policy, published in 1944, gave tentative approval to the 'Keynesian revolution' and pledged future governments to maintain a high and stable level of employment.

Though he referred to Ignorance as one of the Giants on the road to reconstruction, Beveridge had little to say of education. Indeed educational reform arose quite independently out of the work of R.A. Butler, the Conservative President of the Board of Education, and his officials. The 1944 Education Act provided that all children over the age of twelve would receive a separate secondary education free of charge. The school-leaving age was to be raised as soon a possible to fifteen.

The Attlee governments

Since the coalition represented both major parties, Conservative and Labour politicians were committed, in principle, to a common framework of social policy. But the Labour Party sounded far more convincing on social questions than the Conservatives. In the 1945 general election they romped home to victory as the more trustworthy of the parties on social reform.

The welfare programme of the Attlee governments was carried through with great resolve against a background of almost continuous economic crisis. The 1946 Social Insurance Act, introduced by James Griffiths, adopted the Beveridge plan with one bold amendment. It was decided to raise old age pensions to the new level at once, instead of phasing in the increase over 20 years as Beveridge had recommended. But once again the principle of subsistence was eroded. By the time the new scales of benefit were introduced in 1948, their value had been substantially reduced by inflation.

Social insurance was carried through with a minimum of controversy. Not so the other great social measure of the Attlee governments, the National Health Service. Aneurin Bevan, the Minister of Health, aroused the opposition of the Conservative Party by his decision to nationalise the voluntary hospitals. His plans also encountered fierce opposition from the British Medical Association, which claimed that he was seeking to impose dictatorial controls on the medical profession. But the government overcame the opposition and the National Health Service came into operation on the same day as the social security scheme: 5 July 1948.

Much more could be said of Labour's social policy but the overall effect is more important than the individual measures. Apart from a somewhat disappointing record on housing, Labour had carried through its manifesto promises. By 1951 Britain had a comprehensive system of social security, unified health and educational services and – last but not least – full employment. The Welfare State was firmly identified with the Labour Party.

A welfare revolution

It is important to appreciate that, during and after the Second World War, observers of many political persuasions were convinced that Britain was passing through a bloodless 'social revolution' in which the principal feature was a levelling of class distinctions. Politicians of all parties assumed that the main object of welfare reform was to benefit the working classes. At the same time the inclusion of the middle classes in the new Welfare State seemed to put an end to the class basis of social policy.

In his history of the wartime social services, Richard Titmuss argued that the new pattern of social policy was a reflection of the unity and social solidarity of the war years. A similar view was eloquently expressed by Derek Fraser in his *Evolution of the Welfare State* (1973):

> Bombs, unlike employment, knew no social distinctions, and so rich and poor alike were affected in the need for shelter and protection. Food rationing produced common shortages and even the royal family ate spam . . . Though much debased by subsequent political attempts at revivification, the so-called Dunkirk spirit did bring the nation together in a common united purpose,

a remarkable achievement in 1940 considering the divisive policy pursued in the 1930s.[1]

Historiographical reassessment

In recent years historians have begun to challenge this radical-patriotic interpretation of social reform. They argue that Britain in the 1940s was more deeply divided by class and party than previous historians have recognised. Beneath the surface, two nations were contending for the future.

One sign of changing perspectives is a reinterpretation of the impact of evacuation. Historians used to argue that evacuation of women and children from the inner cities revealed to the middle classes the extent of social deprivation and so demonstrated the need for social reform. But as John Macnicol has argued, evacuation could also work in the opposite direction:

> For conservative social observers, it confirmed the view that the bulk of the problems were caused by an incorrigible underclass of personally inadequate 'cultural orphans' for whom a Welfare State could do little. Evacuation thus shows us that the ideological consensus of wartime, so stressed by Titmuss and some historians, was something of a myth.[2]

The equation of social reform with national unity certainly needs clarification. The main factor at work was the increased power of the Labour Party and the trade unions after 1940. Proposals for social reform were an attempt to formulate the terms of a new balance of power between capital and labour. With socialism ruled out as too divisive, welfare took its place as the highest common denominator between the parties. National unity, therefore, took the form of a partial collapse of Conservative resistance to proposals for social reform. But how much did the Conservatives concede?

In his recent study of wartime politics, Kevin Jefferys argues that the Coalition government's discussion of post-war plans was constrained and confined by party conflict.[3] In some areas, he argues, agreement was impossible. In others, like health or employment policy, Coalition proposals were little more than short-term compromises. After their defeat in 1945 the Conservatives were obliged, for electoral reasons, to accept much of the Welfare State in practice. But the conflicting philosophies of the parties remained. The Conservatives were always inclined to return to a more limited Welfare State of means-tested benefits. Labour, on the other hand, viewed the Welfare State as a bridgehead of social equality from which further advances could be made.

The National Health Service

The National Health Service is often cited as the most effective expression of the Labour ideal. But, in a sense, the NHS marked a defeat for Labour policy. Since 1934 the Labour Party had been pledged to introduce a comprehensive service in which general practitioners were employed on a full-time salaried basis in health centres. The British Medical Association, however, was determined to maintain the professional independence of general practioners, and succeeded in imposing its terms. Bevan had to promise that no full-time salaried service would be introduced and health centres made little progress. Whether there was an improvement in the quality of primary health care for the working classes is debatable. According to Charles Webster, the official historian of the NHS:

> The NHS failed to improve the general medical service available to the bulk of the population. The middle classes benefited to some extent, but the lower classes continued to experience a humiliating standard of care. The middle classes were liberated from doctors' fees and they enjoyed the services of the better practitioners, while the lower classes, especially after the introduction of the prescription charge in 1952, continued to receive an inferior service, but for a higher level of payment through taxes and direct charges.[4]

The 1944 Education Act

Like the NHS, the Education Act of 1944 demonstrates the way in which social policy tended to work with the grain of the class structure, rather than against it. When the discussion of educational reform began in 1941 there was some talk of a radical reform of the public schools. Churchill, surprisingly enough, thought that 75% of places in the public schools should be opened up to pupils chosen by local authorities. But R.A. Butler averted radical reform by appointing a committee which ultimately recommended that 25% of places should be made available to state-assisted pupils. Even this modest scheme withered away after 1945.

In the state sector the Education Act was based on the principle of equality of opportunity, which it was thought would enable the working-class scholarship pupil to climb the grammar school ladder. There was, indeed, a small increase in the proportion of working-class pupils at grammar school. Against this must be set the benefits which accrued to the middle classes. Grammar school fees were abolished, and government expenditure on the grammar schools raced ahead of the expenditure on seconary moderns.

Social welfare and national efficiency

Critics of the Welfare State often complained of its failure to rectify social injustice. But they seemed to forget another important test of social policy, which dated back to the turn of the century: national efficiency. How far did social policy equip the nation to compete against other nations? In 1986 Correlli Barnett applied the test of national efficiency to the Welfare State in his book *The Audit of War*.

Barnett argued that the Beveridge report, and the post-war plans of the coalition government, were a mighty step on the road to ruin. The problem confronting Britain in 1945 was how to create wealth as efficiently as possible in order to compete in world markets. The first priority ought to have been the re-equipment of industry and the development of technical education. But the Coalition government capitulated to the 'woolly-minded utopians' who believed in the 'New Jerusalem' of the Welfare State. Industrial investment and training, were sacrificed in favour of social priorities, thus precipitating Britain's post-war economic decline.

The main problem with Barnett's thesis is that the Welfare State was not peculair to Britain. Most countries in western Europe raised their social expenditure after 1945, and the British soon began to lag behind in the proportion of national wealth devoted to social purposes. But this does not entirely dispose of the issue. As José Harris has shown, many other Euopean countries targeted social benefits on the labour force, with the aim of increasing industrial efficiency. The British Welfare State was more generous in its treatment of the old, the chronically sick and the poor, from whom no economic return was to be expected. 'To this extent', Dr Harris writes, 'Barnett's critique of the Welfare State as a hidden cause of Britain's poor economic performance may have some foundation.[5]

The same can be said of his treatment of education reform. When R.A. Butler first contemplated an education bill he listed the reform of technical education as a priority. Much stress was laid on the importance to the British economy of scientific and technical training. A tripartite system of technical, grammar, and modern schools was envisaged. But somehow technical education slipped down the agenda and was all but forgotten. The technical leg of the tripod was never put into place, an omission Barnett attributes to the leading role in the educational establishment of churchmen and classicists.

Full employment

Full employment used to be regarded as the greatest of all the innovations of the 1940s. The 'Keynesian revolution', it was thought, had converted Whitehall to the doctrine of full employment, and provided a foolproof technique for achieving it. But this version of events is no longer very convincing. First, there was prolonged resistance within the Treasury to the adoption of Keynesian ideas. Treasury officials certainly did not regard the 1944 White Paper on employment policy as a commitment to 'full' employment: they expected unemployment levels of up to 8.5%. Secondly, Keynesianism was a double-sided doctrine. Though it prescribed an expansion of demand to prevent a slump, it also prescribed the restriction of demand to prevent inflation. By the late 1940s the Treasury was converted to Keynesianism as a means of enforcing balanced budgets and cuts in public expenditure. Keynesianism, in this sense, was a corset restricting the growth of the social services.[6] A third point follows. Full employment was not the result of a 'Keynesian revolution', but of the boom in private investment after 1945.

Conclusion

Half a century after the Beveridge Report it is clear that the Second World War raised expectations that were never fulfilled. Some of the most radical ideas of the period, like Beveridge's plan for subsistence level benefits, were never implemented. The class structure proved more enduring, and the power of the state more limited, than radical reformers imagined. Social reform had little impact on the position of women. Yet revisionists should beware of revising away the 1940s. The welfare reforms of the period were an impressive attempt to create a post-war settlement based on new conceptions of social justice. They did succeed in raising the living standards of the poor, and the social status of the working classes as a whole.

Notes

(1) Fraser, D. *The Evolution of the Welfare State* (Macmillan, 1973) pp. 193–4.
(2) Macnicol, J. 'The effect of the evacuation of schoolchildren on official attitudes to State intervention' in Harold L. Smith (ed.) *War and Social Change* (Manchester University Press, 1986).
(3) Jefferys, R. *The Churchill Coalition and Wartime Politics 1940–1945* (Manchester University Press, 1990)
(4) Webster, C. 'Doctors, public service and profit: General Practitioners and the National Health Service', *TRHS* 5th series Vol. 40, p. 214.
(5) Harris, J. 'Enterprise and welfare states: a comparative perspective, *TRHS* 5th series Vol. 40, p. 183.
(6) Middleton, R. 'Keynes's legacy for post-war economic management' in T. Gorst, L. Johnman and W.S. Lucas (eds) *Post-war Britain 1945–1964: Themes and Perspectives* (Pinter, 1989) p. 31.

Paul Addison teaches History at the University of Edinburgh. He is the author of *The Road to 1945* and *Churchill on the Home Front 1900–55*.

Correlli Barnett

War and Economic Performance

Few books receive the wide public acclaim of Correlli Barnett's The Audit of War *(Macmillan, 1986). But how sound are Barnett's arguments?*

The audit of war, as documented in the then secret files of the Cainbet and its committees and the various war production ministries, makes clear that 'the British disease' as we now recognise it was rampant even in wartime. The truth is that wartime Britain stands like a missing link between the long decline from the 1870s to the 1930s, and the renewed slide from the early 1950s onwards, once foreign rivals had got off the floor and recovered from defeat and occupation.

To start with, the bare statistics reveal the existence of the 'disease' in 1939–45 across the gamut of industries, from old Victorian 'heavies' like coal to new high-tech ones like aircraft and machine-tools. In aircraft British peak annual productivity in structure weight per employee was only four-fifths of German, but less than half of American. Take the Spitfire, that great British legend. Partly as a consequence of a design derived from a one-off racing seaplane and ill-adapted to mass production, it took three times the manhours to build a Spitfire Mark VC than its equivalent, the Messerschmitt 109G.

Given the desperate need for maximum output, it is not surprising that various ministries – Supply, Production, Aircraft Production, the Admiralty – carried out urgent field investigations to try to find out what was wrong. And the reports of the investigating teams reveal some now familiar villains. The first was the low average quality of British management.

In the coal industry, for example, a Cabinet Committee in 1942 looking into the reasons for falling production and falling productivity heard expert witnesses tell it: 'It is well known that for some years it has been found difficult to attract to the Industry a sufficient number of well educated young men likely to develop into first-class Mining Engineers.' Instead, there were too many 'practical men', able to run a colliery on traditional lines from day to day by rule-of-thumb, but quite incapable of planning and directing a large-scale modern colliery operation as a single integrated machine. In the shipbuilding industry, detailed field investigations in 1942 found a management often elderly and timid, deeply resistant to new methods of standardised prefabricated construction. According to the author of one report:

> The planning of the work and the operation of the shipyard does not appear to have made much progress in the last twenty years. The work proceeds with the maximum effort, and methodical handling of material is rare

But things were not always much better with the management of the aircraft industry either. A Whitehall memorandum in November 1944 averred:

> Probably the most outstanding single cause of failing to reach a maximum production efficiency in wartime is scarcity of skilled management.

At worst, the aircraft industry's management could be ghastly indeed. Vickers Armstrong (Aircraft) at Weybridge, a team of five Ministry of Production experts, found that the assistant to the production manager was a solicitor with no engineering experience, while the production manager refused to delegate and insisted on trying to control everything himself. According to this team of experts, there existed 'no system of line production throughout the whole organisation.' This was not an exceptional case: the development of the jet engine had to be removed from Rovers, according to an unpublished official study, because of the 'chaotic condition of the production organisation'. In any case Glosters, the makers of the airframe, were, according to the same study, equally chaotic.

By contrast, a British aircraft industry mission in 1943 to the US reported thus on management in the American aircraft industry:

> The various production operations are broken down into stages and planned more elaborately in America than in this country. Much time and effort is put into preparation work of scheduling, process planning, machine loading, labour loading and shop layout, and this is carried out in greater detail in America than is customary in many of our factories. This is considered to be an essential part of obtaining efficient production.

But, of course, such an approach required plenty of highly-qualified production engineers, not just the shop-trained ex-apprentice typical of British line management.

British management in all industries also proved inept, and weak in leading its workforce, which served only to worsen the other great cause of lagging British productivity – the obstructiveness of the trade unions and the lack of commitment of the workers. There was a continual guerilla warfare of unofficial strikes, mostly wildcat, and go-slows. There was also a near universal tendency to shorten shifts and lengthen breaks at both ends. These particular symptoms of the British disease, which became so notorious in the 1960s and 1970s, are bluntly documented in the war years of the 1940s and tabulated in the weekly 'strike chart' kept by the Ministry of Labour and National Service. Days lost through strikes in Britain were higher every year from 1941 to 1945 than in 1938, the last full year of peacetime. Coal was far and away the worst offender, with no fewer than 1.2 million mandays and 2 million tons of coal lost in the first quarter of 1944 alone. Usually a coal strike was about wages – the coalminer's place in the industrial pecking order. But one local strike in 1944, costing 1,000 tons of production, was simply because the miners wanted to get rid of a canteen lady. However, strikes were only the visible manifestation of a deeper disgruntlement. In 1944 a visiting team of American mining experts reported that the key to the British problem of lagging production and productivity was:

> the bad feeling and antagonism which pervade the industry and which manifests itself in low morale, non-cooperation and indifference. In almost every district we visited, miners' leaders and mine owners complained of men leaving the mines early, failure to clear the faces and voluntary absenteeism.

With shipbuilding and ship-repairing, 'who does what' stoppages abounded, even though Britain stood in desperate danger of losing the Battle of the Atlantic for want of warships and merchant ships to replace those sunk by U-boats. In the words of a Ministry of Labour memorandum in October 1943:

> Few industries require the skills of so many different types of craftsmen (each necessarily working in the same confined area) or experience so much difficulty in keeping them continuously employed; it frequently happens that some of the skilled craftsmen are unable to get their work through to time whilst other types of craftsmen are insufficiently occupied. Owing to demarcation restrictions, however, the latter cannot help the former, although technically equipped to do so.

In unrelenting pursuit of such absurdities, worthy of a weird land of nonsense visited by Gulliver, the Amalgamated Engineering Union and the Boilermakers' Society refused to allow appropriately skilled members of the National Union of Railwaymen to work in shipyards; the Electricians' Trade Union in one shipyard refused to work with a non-union electrician, and threatened to strike; and the Boilermakers went on strike in December 1944 over a dispute with the Shipwrights' Union over who should operate a flame-cutting machine. Even day-to-day interchangeability, like an electrician boring the hole for his own wiring, was not achieved on any scale.

The craft unions in the shipyards also fought to the last to prevent the introduction of new technology and 'dilution' by unskilled labour; and it was the Boilermaker's Society that provided the Old Guard in this largely successful last stand. In the words of a Ministry of Labour official in May 1943, 'Whenever dilution is raised, we seem to be brought up against this ghostly squad of unemployed boilermakers.' When and where pneumatic riveting replaced hand-riveting, employers (feeble as they were) and unions agreed that an additional man, as needed on pre-war hand-riveting, should also be employed. As a Mass-Observation Report noted at the time, this chap 'has nothing at all to do now, except sit all day beside the riveters. He draws full wages.'

And shipyard workers were not notorious for zeal either, as reported by one investigating committee in 1942:

> We have evidence of a lack of discipline, particularly among the younger men, and a reluctance to work agreed overtime, and our attention was drawn to what has become a custom whereby workers delay starting work until 10 or 15 minutes after the due time and begin making their way to the gates 10 or 15 minutes before stopping time.

One should remember that all this was occurring at a time when Britain's very survival depended on ships and the sea. If British shipbuilding could not get its act together even under the spur of total war, when would it?

Yet it should not be thought that things were so much better in modern industries like aircraft or machine-tools or light engineering in general. As early as 1941 sloth in aircraft factories was causing anxiety. A report on de Havilland at Castle Bromwich, for instance, found 'a marked absence of discipline', 'slackness', and 'difficulty in controlling shop stewards.' In April 1943 the new Production Efficiency Board visited Coventry and reported that there would be no need for extra labour if only the existing labour force did its stuff. But timings and prices for piecework made it possible to enjoy 'high earnings without a corresponding high effort.' As the Board wrote:

> In each factory there is evidence of slackness and lack of discipline. Operators are slow in starting work at the beginning of each shift and after each break, and there is a complete stoppage of work from 15 to 30 minutes before each break

Meantime, the craft unions hung on to their demarcations and restrictive practices in the aircraft industry, despite the Restoration of Trade Practices Act of 1940, which guaranteed that the privileges of the craft unions everywhere would be fully restored after the war. Of all absurdities, the sheetmetal unions sought to maintain that because for centuries metal had been shaped by craftsmen banging away with hand tools, then metal shaping for a Spitfire or Lancaster by the power press and automatic tool in a mass-production factory must be rated as craftsmen's work, and manned and paid as such.

It is, therefore, no wonder that the rise in aircraft output during the war was achieved not by revolutionary improvement in productivity, but by simply deploying over 100,000 extra machine tools and over a million extra workers.

Thus we see that the fat, flabby, deeply conservative industrial economy so familiar in the post-war era was well and truly in business while the nation was fighting for its very life. In fact, it was even encouraged by wartime conditions. Firms on government contracts were subject to no discipline of international or even home-market competition, but swanned comfortably along on a 'cost-plus' basis – a fixed but certain profit on top of whatever their costs turned out to be. On the other hand, wartime 'full-employment' to the extent of actual poaching of scarce labour decisively swung the balance of industrial leverage from managements to unions and workforce, so leaving no effective sanctions to spur efficiency and effort. Thus British industry emerged from the war in the armchair posture it was to retain until the late 1970s.

Yet the audit of war does not only expose the shortcomings of management and workforce. It reveals other enduring features of 'the British disease' as well as a cripplingly narrow base in high-tech industries and skills, a concomitant difficulty in 'technology transfer' from original invention into series production of kit, and therefore a strong dependence on imports of advanced technology. Sound familiar?

To take a basic capability of an advanced industrial economy – machine tools. The British machine-tool industry was quite unable to tool Britain's new wartime factories, whether aircraft, munitions, general engineering, or radio and radar. In the first place its total output was too small. Whereas Germany easily tooled all her own factories, Britain had to turn to America for vast quantities of machines – in the peak years of 1940 and 1941, amounting to half of Britain's own output. But dependence on America was much greater in respect of highly sophisticated advanced types of tool. In 1942 imports of automatic lathes were 2½ times Britain's own production; of turret lathes, 3 times; of vertical drillers, 2 times. In 1941 Britain found herself totally dependent on America for over 20 types of machine tool. Thus British wartime output of high-tech products, from aircraft to radar, guns to instruments, would have been impossible without massive imports of US tools.

It is a key part of Britain's national myth about her wonderful wartime technological achievement that British scientists were responsible for the development of successive generations of radar, of electronic target-finding devices for Bomber Command like Oboe and H2S, and such other devices as radio-proximity fuses for anti-aircraft shell. And there is no question that British original R&D was brilliant. But the problem lay in the gulf between these scientists and the industry that had got to manufacture their inventions. Professor Tizard reported in May 1942 that there were 2,500 radio engineers in government employ, as against 864 in the industry itself. In February 1943 there were 541 research workers in government establishments, as against only 236 in the entire radio industry. On basic research, the staff at TRE numbered 34, as against only 15 in all the radio firms. The gap in expertise was the worse because the brilliant boffins for their part had little concept of production problems.

The inferiority of the British industrial machine to the German or American machine during the Second World War reflects, however, deeper shortcomings in Britain as an industrial society. Above all, the shortcomings were in education and training. Just before the Second World War Germany was turning out over 1,900 graduate engineers a year, as against a British figure of some 700. The German figure for mechanical engineers alone, at 662, almost equalled the British output for all kinds of engineers. On top of that, the superb German engineer schools produced over 2,000 fully qualified practical engineers. The German output of electrical engineers in the one year 1937 (a key category, remember) at 448 amounted to more than half the cumulative British total of 781 for the fourteen years 1925–39. Unlike Germany or America, Britain then had no business schools.

Now let's look at education and training in 1937 in regard to middle management. Britain had just 20,000 youngsters in part-time further education in 1937; Germany had over 1,800,000. In full-time vocational and technical training of all kinds between the ages of 16 and 21, Germany had proportionately more than twice as many young people as Britain. Whereas in many German industries there was 100% in-job vocational training, in Britain the figure was about 10%. Throughout the war the production ministries complained about the deep reluctance of British firms, even in advanced technologies like aircraft, to train their workforce.

When you turn to ordinary school education, the picture is just as depressing. Proportionately twice as many German youngsters than British stayed on through secondary school, to the age of 18; proportionately 2½ times the number of German youngsters obtained the *Zeugnis der Reife* than British obtained the Higher Schools Certificate. And, finally, of the grand total of 663,000 school-leavers in Britain in 1937 from all kinds of state school and at all ages, only 13,000 had received any kind of career preparation whatsoever. And Butler's vaunted Education Act of 1944 did virtually nothing for technical and further education: it was simply a legislative gate opening on to an empty site on which too little was to be built too late.

Correlli Barnett was Keeper of Archives at Churchill College, Cambridge.

Kevin Jefferys
Attlee Governments 1945–51

How radical were the post-war Labour governments and how constrained were they by the difficult circumstances they faced?

Historians are agreed upon the importance of the post-war Labour governments in shaping modern Britain. After a landslide election victory in 1945, the administration led by Clement Attlee presided over a series of far-reaching changes, both at home and abroad. In domestic affairs, attention centred on the introduction of the Welfare State and a 'mixed' economy. Overseas, these years witnessed the first phase of a transition from Empire to Commonwealth, and saw Britain reinforce its 'special relationship' with the United States in order to counter the emerging threat of Soviet expansionism. By the time Attlee's second, short-lived government of 1950–51 left office, Labour could claim much of the credit for a new political order: a 'post-war settlement' that was to remain in place for a generation to come. But judgements on the end result have been more mixed. Was this, as adherents of Thatcherism in the 1980s suggested, a time when the powers of the state were over-extended and individual initiative undermined? Conversely, was this a period when the opportunity to transform capitalism fundamentally was lost, because of the timidity of ministers? Or, as others still have argued, did Labour achieve all that was possible in the circumstances?

Victory in 1945

The Second World War had transformed British politics. As the defeat of Nazi Germany became assured in 1945, the 'national unity' government of Conservative and Labour forces, formed in the emergency of 1940, finally broke apart. Winston Churchill, Britain's inspirational wartime Premier, called on the electorate to return him as the head of a new Conservative administration. Among politicians and commentators, it was widely assumed that Churchill would sweep back to power in the general election of 1945, just as Lloyd George had triumphed in 1918 as 'the man who won the war'. But such predictions proved to be wildly inaccurate. Churchill's immense popularity as a war leader was offset by his misjudgement of the electorate's desire to create a 'New Jerusalem' – a theme made central in Labour's wartime pronouncements. As the election results came through, it became apparent that a major shift in popular opinion had taken place. At the last pre-war election, held in 1935, Labour trailed the Tory-dominated National government by over 200 parliamentary seats. In 1945, however, Labour secured nearly half the popular vote, winning 393 seats, compared with 213 for the Conservatives. Hence it was not Churchill but the relatively unknown Attlee who became the nation's first post-war leader.

Attlee was certainly an unlikely figurehead for a new era. According to his many detractors, 'Clem the Clam' as he was once called, was a modest man with much to be modest about. But as became increasingly clear, Attlee's clipped tones concealed great inner confidence. Those who worked with him were to reflect that his combination of 'honesty, common sense and intelligence' made him an ideal foil for the powerful personalities around the cabinet table. Of these, Ernest Bevin stood out as Foreign Secretary.

With his great physical presence and bullying manner, Bevin was a key figure in the government's fortunes. He refused to take part in isolated challenges to Attlee's leadership and his alliance with the Prime Minister ensured firm direction on matters of foreign and domestic policy. The omens for Labour were thus better than Attlee's critics implied. The Prime Minister quickly assembled a talented team of ministers, hardened by wartime experience, and he came to power with a detailed programme backed by both a united Labour movement and the electorate. The only clouds on the horizon came from external economic forces: would the huge cost of the war prevent Labour from fulfilling its ambitions?

Domestic reform

Britain had lost almost a quarter of its entire national wealth in the fight against Hitler. Labour ministers, assisted by the negotiation of a large loan from the US, were nevertheless determined to press ahead with their full domestic programme. Much of the lead in the early days was taken by another leading member of the inner cabinet, Hugh Dalton, who became Chancellor of the Exchequer. Dalton's radical instincts – and his overbearing manner – inspired great hostility on the opposition benches. Churchill had once been interrupted in the war by loud bellowing from an adjoining room. 'It's Dalton speaking from Glasgow', an official explained. 'Why doesn't he use the telephone?' asked Churchill. It was the Chancellor who consciously shaped economic policy in order to assist ordinary working families, most of whom were still suffering hardships associated with rationing and war shortages. Food subsidies were kept high in order to hold down living costs, taxation bit hardest on the better off, and regional policy was vigorously pursued to help ensure that there was no return to high unemployment in the industrial blackspots of the 1930s.

The most distinctive element of the government's economic strategy was its programme of nationalisation. Labour had long been committed to public ownership, both as a means of creating service industries, operated not solely for shareholder's profits but for the benefit of the wider community, and as a means of redeeming industries such as coal that had proved inefficient under private ownership. These claims had a strong appeal in 1945, coming at the end of a war in which the state had assumed a greater responsibility over the national economy. In consequence, Herbert Morrison – the government's organisational chief – assumed responsibility for introducing an extensive programme of public ownership, covering the civil aviation, coal, transport and electricity industries. Although the opposition at first put up only token resistance, as Conservative morale recovered in 1947–48, so there were increasingly strong attacks on Labour's interference with the free market economy.

In social policy, the government also moved quickly to introduce a new system of universal social security benefits, based upon the principle of the wartime Beveridge Report. But the most radical policies were associated with the Minister of Health, Aneurin Bevan. In an effort to favour working-class families, he shifted priorities in house building from the private to the local authority sector; four out of five houses constructed under the Attlee government were council properties. Altogether over a million homes were built in the six years after the war. Although there was frustration with the initial pace of reform, this was partly due to the priority accorded to establishing a National Health Service, which for the first time introduced free treatment to hospital and general practitioner services. Bevan was bitterly opposed by the British Medical Association and by the Conservative opposition, which voted against the 1946 NHS Act. But his achievement was beyond question. The health service was to be the most popular, and the most enduring, of Labour's welfare reforms.

On the defensive

After its initial surge of enthusiasm and legislative progress, the government began to run into difficulties. 1947 witnessed first a 'winter crisis', when severe weather and a fuel shortage combined to produce a temporary industrial standstill; and subsequently a 'convertibility crisis', sparked off when sterling came under intense pressure on the foreign exchange. Ministers were now faced with an erosion of public confidence. By the end of the year the Tories had edged ahead in the opinion polls for the first time since Attlee came to power, and the Prime Minister had accepted the resignation of his Chancellor, worn down by the traumas of the past few months. 1947 thus marked a point of transition: from the confidence of the early days to a period when ministers used the language of restraint and 'consolidation'. This 'age of austerity' became closely identified with the figure of Stafford Cripps, Dalton's successor at the Treasury, a vegetarian teetotaller noted for a work rate that included three hours at his desk before breakfast. Hoping for similar commitment from the nation, he continued with a wartime-style 'fair shares' policy of food rationing, even though this meant ever-lengthening queues to obtain food of dubious quality. Cripps was convinced that only increased productivity would allow Britain to become a progressively fairer society. He therefore moved away from any remaining notions of socialist planning, tightened the belt on welfare expenditure, and devalued sterling in the face of fresh economic difficulties in order to maintain an export drive.

Aside from external forces, the government also found itself confronted with an increasingly revitalised opposition. The Conservative claim that scarcities in the shops were due to socialist inefficiency struck a popular chord in the run-up to a general election, finally called in February 1950. Labour allegations that the post-war settlement would be threatened by the return of Churchill were strenuously denied by the Conservatives, who emphasised their broad acceptance of welfare reform. In the event, a record turnout helped to ensure that Labour polled more votes than it had in 1945. But so too did the Conservatives. The results revealed a swing against Labour of 2.9% (compared with 12% against the Tories in 1945), leaving Attlee with a tiny majority of six seats in the House of Commons. Regional trends pointed to the underlying causes of this outcome. Broadly working-class constituencies, especially in the north and west, demonstrated their satisfaction by remaining solidly behind the government. But Labour lost ground in seats with a preponderance of middle-class voters, notably in the South East, where austerity was a primary cause of voter disaffection. 'We proclaimed a just policy of fair shares', reflected Hugh Dalton, 'but the complaint was not so much that shares were unfair, but that they were too small.'

The 1950–51 government

With hindsight, the second Attlee administration looked doomed from the outset. Dalton saw the 1950 result as the worst of all possible outcomes, leaving Labour in office but 'without authority or power'. In practice, however, ministers were primarily blown off course by the unexpected outbreak of the Korean War in June 1950. With memories of appeasement fresh, the government committed itself to a massive increase in defence spending in order to back the fight against Communist North Korea. This not only placed an immense strain on the economy; it also provoked the first major split in Labour ranks since 1945. Nye Bevan refused to accept the case put by Hugh Gaitskell – who became Chancellor after Cripps resigned through ill-health – that defence commitments could only be met by economising on domestic spending, including the health service. Bevan's resignation over the imposition of health service charges symbolised an emerging division between left and right over future party strategy that was to persist for many years. At the time, it reinforced the impression of an administration that had lost its sense of direction. When Attlee decided to call another election in October 1951, there were few signs of the enthusiasm and unity of 1945.

The 1951 election campaign was fought on similar lines to that of 1950. Labour's emphasis on the consolidation of post-war advances was countered by Conservative promises to 'set the people free' from socialist bureaucracy. The outcome was a further small swing to the Tories, sufficient to give Churchill a 17-seat parliamentary majority. Most of the electorate voted the same way as in 1950. For the crucial minority who did switch allegiance – especially in the South East where the Conservatives gained 20 seats – unsatisfied material ambitions proved more important than Labour's internal divisions. Ironically, by again piling up huge majorities in its industrial heartlands, Labour actually won more votes, if fewer seats, than the Tories. Some stalwarts such as Dalton consequently assumed a return to power would soon follow voter disillusionment with Churchill. In the event, most of Labour's generation of 1945 were never again to return to high office.

Attlee's legacy

In looking back on the immediate post-war years, those who, like Correlli Barnett, lament the priority given to welfare reform have perhaps underestimated the desire of the British electorate to create a New Jerusalem. Labour was elected in 1945 precisely because of its commitment to reforms that ordinary voters felt had been too long denied. Left-wing critics, conversely, have argued that there was too little rather than too much socialism during the Attlee years. Britain, it has been noted, remained a profoundly unequal and class-ridden society, in which 1% of the population still owned 50% of all private capital. Such a critique, however, presupposes that a more radical agenda was readily available in the late 1940s, when in reality the small number of dissident Labour backbenchers were themselves imprecise about what 'more socialism' might entail in practice. In later years, even those who grumbled at the time came to share the view that democratic socialism had proved itself to be a success. As Ian Mikardo put it in his memoirs *Back-Bencher*:

> In those difficult years we sought to answer, for the first time in the recorded history of man, the first question a man ever asked, Am I my brother's keeper?, and we said Yes, brother, you are your brother's keeper.

Most of the party faithful were certainly satisfied with what had been achieved when Labour left office in 1951. On the world stage, Ernest Bevin's endeavours, especially in helping to create NATO, had left Britain with a degree of flexibility and security that would have been envied by policy-makers in the 1930s. In domestic politics, the government could claim credit for shaping economic recovery. Low levels of unemployment clearly owed much to a revival of world trade after the war, though similar opportunities after the First World War had not prevented a short boom being followed by deep recession. Alec Cairncross's exhaustive study of the main economic indicators concludes that, in spite of the intractability of many features of Britain's 'industrial disease', this was a record that could hardly have been bettered. Economic recovery was also vital in enabling the government to provide tangible welfare benefits of a type that had hitherto been denied to the majority. For the young, free secondary education became a right for the first time; for the elderly, pensions approximated as never before to the level of a living income. If much remained to be done in reducing inequalities, party activists were convinced that important steps had been taken in the right direction, and taken moreover in the face of both economic hardship and political resistance.

At the time, however, Labour could not rest on its laurels. At least three difficulties for the party remained unresolved as Attlee left Downing Street. In the first place, Labour had reinforced its working-class electoral base, but had lost the confidence of many within the middle class who had contributed to the 'high tide' of 1945. This problem was crucial if the Conservatives were to be dislodged from power, and was linked with a second anxiety. The successful implementation of Labour's traditional programme left the obvious question: what was to be put in its place? For some, consolidation of gains made since 1945 was essential; only moderate policies would keep on board those more concerned with material prosperity than with the fading wartime ethos of fair shares. But for others, consolidation was not enough in a party committed to radical change. This problem, of constructing a new programme appropriate for the 1950s, tied in with a final difficulty: that of the age profile of the party leadership. Labour's senior ministers had made their mark, but were by now part of an elderly political generation, unlikely to provide the innovative thinking necessary to reinvigorate the party. But the main representatives of a younger generation, Bevan and Gaitskell, had split the party before the debate about future priorities had really got under way. These three factors – the need to attract more cross-class support, the void at the heart of party policy and the disastrous Bevan-Gaitskell dispute – all helped to cloud Attlee's legacy. The years 1945–51 had been Labour's 'finest hour', but it came at a price.

Further Reading

Cairncross, A. *Years of Recovery: British Economic Policy 1945–51* (Methuen, 1985).
Eatwell, R. *The 1945–51 Labour Governments* (Batsford, 1979).
Hennessy, P. *Never Again: Britain 1945–51* (Jonathan Cape, 1992).
Jefferys, K. *The Attlee Governments 1945–51* (Longman, 1992).
Morgan, K.O. *Labour in Power 1945–51* (Oxford University Press, 1984).
Pelling, H. *The Labour Governments 1945–51* (Macmillan, 1984).
Saville, J. *The Labour Movement in Britain* (Faber and Faber, 1988).
Tiratsoo, N. (ed.) *The Attlee Years* (Pinter Publishers, 1991).

Kevin Jefferys is Senior Lecturer in Contemporary History at the University of Plymouth.

Nick Tiratsoo

The Attlee Years Revisited

Nick Tiratsoo offers a critical appraisal of many of the traditional views of the post-war Labour government, and particularly of the notion that these years marked the beginning of a 'post-war consensus'.

The Labour administration, led by Clement Attlee, which governed Britain between 1945 and 1951, has been the subject of much controversy amongst historians. This was the first period of majority socialist rule in British history and it is usually remembered for some great reforms – the nationalisation programme and the creation of the Welfare State. Opinion is divided, however, on the question of whether these reforms had a beneficial or a damaging impact on Britain's long-term development. Some have defended the government's record, but others continue to see the late 1940s as years of wasted opportunity. In this article, I want to outline each of the different approaches to the Attlee period and then argue for some new thinking on various aspects of the issues raised.

Historiography

Not surprisingly, the most positive assessments of the Attlee years have come from those who are generally sympathetic to Labour's overall aims. The historians Paul Addison and Kenneth Morgan explain the party's 1945 election triumph in terms of a broad consensus for change that had developed during the war. They then go on to characterise Labour's subsequent performance in office as decisive and noteworthy: the picture presented is of a united administration with a coherent programme, in step with public opinion, and making a break with the past over issues from health care to empire. Labour eventually fell, in this view, because it ran out of steam, but a measure of the government's enormous impact can be seen from the bold imprint it left on the following decades. Indeed, Attlee's society remained unchanged in many ways until the advent of Margaret Thatcher.[1]

Inevitably, such positive conclusions are challenged by those with other political loyalties. Left-wing critics of Labour, such as Ralph Miliband and John Saville, argue that Attlee, like MacDonald before and Wilson after, promised much but delivered little. They believe that Labour was elected on a dramatic and radical popular upsurge in 1945, but subsequently proved something of a damp squib. The government mouthed the rhetoric of socialism and enacted some real reforms (particularly over welfare) but in the end became too concerned with re-stabilising capitalism and too involved in America's Cold War. Defeat at the 1951 election was inevitable, because many working-class voters were disgusted at this catalogue of betrayals. The whole, sorry story confirms Labour's historic inadequacy as a party of real change.[2]

Those on the right of politics have also been highly critical of the Attlee years, often drawing on insights first presented in Correlli Barnett's widely influential *The Audit of War* (1986). Here, the conclusions of the Addison-Morgan view are broadly accepted, but placed in a very different and highly pessimistic light. Thus, Barnett agrees that Labour's aims were supported by a majority of the electorate in 1945, but he believes that this occurred because many were misled in their thinking about Britain's future by utopian social reformers like Beveridge. Similarly, he accepts that the country was indeed decisively changed by 1951, yet he sees this as disastrous, since the reforms prioritised social improvements at the expense of long-term economic health. For Barnett, in fact, Britain took the wrong fork in 1945 and Labour bears much of the responsibility. The country needed new homes and hospitals, but these should only have been provided (as in Germany) after the re-creation of an efficient industrial base.

At this point, the reader may well be concluding that there can be little more of interest to say about the Attlee years. Historians may have disagreed about interpretation, but they must surely have examined all the substantive issues. However, I want to argue in what follows that this impression is wrong and that the historiography is not as comprehensive as it appears. In particular, I want to challenge two important judgments which appear in many of the existing accounts.

Labour: party of industrial modernisation?

As will already have become clear, it is generally agreed by all the various schools of historians that Labour's essential purpose after 1945 was welfare reform. Obviously, this common assessment contains more than a grain of truth. On the other hand, we should not be misled into seeing Labour as simply utopian, prepared to pursue its objective of a fairer society regardless of cost or consequence. Attlee and his ministers did want to create a Welfare State, but they recognised that their plans would only be feasible if the British economy prospered. The consequence was a decision to pursue a kind of 'supply-side socialism'.[3] To understand what this meant in practice, we must return to 1945 and the new administration's own evaluation of the possibilities and difficulties before it.

Labour took office recognising that reform would not be easy. Creating socialism required resources but as everyone knew, Britain had been virtually bankrupted by the war and now faced a massive balance of payments problem. Obviously, consumer expenditure would have to remain closely controlled using the wartime rationing system. An American loan, too, seemed inevitable in order to gain breathing space. However, the real solution to the country's problems had to be increased production, particularly of goods suitable for export. How could this be achieved? There was clearly little scope for adding extra inputs of capital or labour in the short run, and so efforts would have to be concentrated on making existing resources more efficient. Most senior Labour ministers had been involved in the war economy and they knew that many British companies were technically backward and blighted by 'us and them' attitudes on the shop floor. Labour's ability to progress, therefore, seemed to depend on some kind of industrial modernisation.

How were such perceptions turned into policy over the ensuing years? Some sectors were judged either too backward or too run down for piecemeal reform and so were taken into public ownership. Nevertheless, the Attlee government always recognised that this solution would only be feasible in a minority of cases, and so ministers also produced a fairly imaginative programme of measures aimed squarely at the private sector. An early initiative here, launched soon after the 1945 election, involved the creation of working parties (composed of employers, trade unionists and outside experts) which were charged with investigating individual industries and recommending improvements. Other action followed on a number of different fronts. The government recognised that managers played a key role in every industrial undertaking and so created the British Institute of Management in 1948 to raise standards. Moreover, it enthusiastically backed the Anglo-American Council on Productivity, a body set up under the Marshall Plan which sent many British industrialists and workers to America so that they could report back to their colleagues about the most modern techniques and practices. Finally, Labour was involved, too, in improving industrial relations. Typical, for example, was the official campaign to encourage joint production committees in individual firms – forums where employers and employees could thrash out their differences and thus hopefully achieve a common purpose.

This was, all told, an impressive experiment in industrial policy and it clearly brought a number of important benefits, not least a significant upward trend in labour productivity figures. Nevertheless, it is also evident that much less was achieved during these years than some had hoped for. In part, this was because Labour's objectives on productivity clashed with its policies elsewhere. Thus, firms often found difficulty in reconciling simultaneous exhortations to improve efficiency and export at all costs. On the other hand, some of the government's problems certainly occurred because of deliberate obstruction, and here the employers were most to blame. Labour continually stressed that it aimed to enhance rather than control industry, but British business remained for the most part hostile to these advances, believing that the suggested measure of union consultation would fatally compromise 'the manager's right to manage', and fearing that any degree of state involvement must inevitably end in nationalisation. In this situation, Labour too often became bogged down in long drawn-out guerilla struggles, as it tried to drag recalcitrant industrialists forward against their will. Labour's good intentions were not enough, in many cases, to overcome the business world's belief that it alone knew best.

Labour: the people's party?

This conclusion immediately raises a second important issue. Labour had a big majority in Parliament during these years, and it is obviously puzzling to find a vested interest effectively blocking an important set of policies. Why had Attlee and his ministers allowed themselves to get in to this situation? Were they, perhaps, as Miliband and Saville argue, less interested in pushing for real change than their rhetoric might lead us to believe?

To answer these questions, we need to look very closely at the balance of power in Britain after 1945. Most historians, as has been shown, consider Labour to have been almost unassailable until late into its term of office, but there are good reasons for thinking that the party's room for manoeuvre was not nearly as generous as some have imagined. This point can be amplified by looking briefly at events during and after the war.

For many historians, the war acted as a great catalyst on British society, dissolving the old order and encouraging a new radicalism. Involvement in a people's war, it is alleged, made many different groups in the population determined that the experiences of the 1930s should never be repeated. However, a closer inspection of the evidence suggests that the war was generally rather less subversive than has been claimed. Women were not suddenly 'liberated' by working in factories, for example. In fact, most were given the worst jobs, and could not wait to return home as a consequence. Nor was the experience of service life commonly radicalising. Some clearly saw themselves as involved in anti-fascist struggle, but for many others the real point was to defend 'King and Country'. Everywhere, the most common experience of war was disruption – of home, family, job and leisure time. In this situation, when people in Britain started to think about what they wanted from the peace, their choices tended to be fairly prosaic – a home with a garden, steady employment and some relaxation and quiet.

How did this mood shape the outcome of the 1945 election? Most working-class people, of course, voted Labour; however, they did so not because the party promised socialism but rather because it spoke of new houses and full employment. Nevertheless, plenty of ordinary voters, even in 1945, liked the Conservatives better, and, in fact, centre and right parties taken together polled marginally better than the left. After the contest, Labour leaders gradually became aware of a truth that some latter-day historians have too often forgotten – with the British system, Parliamentary majorities can sometimes be poor guides to relative party strengths, let alone actual popular feeling on matters of political detail.

In many ways, developments over the next six years continued to underline this message. A majority of working-class voters remained loyal to Labour but what they liked about the party, as before, were the concrete commitments on welfare provision rather than the abstracts of socialist rhetoric. However, it would, again, be foolish to overestimate Labour strength. The Conservatives had engineered a real recovery by the late 1940s, based on a genuinely popular critique of state regulation in all its forms. Indeed, the vitality of their appeal was amply demonstrated at the 1951 poll, which Labour lost not because of any sense of betrayal amongst its erstwhile supporters but rather because of its failure to match the Tory vision of a property-owning democracy.[4]

Considered against this background, to sum up, we can readily understand why Labour was somewhat diffident about treating the employers too roughly in the 1940s. The government wanted industry to modernise, but it also needed exports. At the same time, everyone recognised that confrontations over issues like productivity would hardly galvanise Labour supporters. In this situation, the only possible strategy open to ministers was one of persuasion and compromise, regardless of the accompanying frustrations.

Some conclusions

What general conclusions emerge from this discussion? A great deal has been written about the Attlee years but it seems to me that much of this literature misleads in some important respects. The Labour government, as has been shown here, was a considerably more rounded administration than is generally accepted; it pursued welfare reform, certainly, but did not ignore industrial modernisation. However, we must also recognise that policy successes and failures were to some extent determined by factors outside Labour's control. Britain did not 'go socialist' in 1945, and in many ways remained a very conservative (and Conservative) country. These points should always be remembered when making final judgments about Attlee's overall performance.

Notes

(1) Addison, P. *The Road to 1945* (Cape, 1975) and Morgan, K.O. *Labour in Power 1945–51* (Oxford University Press, 1984).
(2) Milibrand, R. *Parliamentary Socialism* (Faber, 1961) and Saville, J. *The Labour Movement in Britain* (Faber, 1988).
(3) Tomlinson, J. 'Mr Attlee's supply-side socialism', *Economic History Review*, Vol. 46 (1993) pp.1–22.
(4) See, on the politics of the 1940s, various contributions in Smith, H. (ed.) *War and Social Change* (Manchester University Press, 1986) and Tiratsoo, N. (ed.) *The Attlee Years* (Pinter, 1991).

Nick Tiratsoo teaches at the Centre for the Study of Social History, the University of Warwick. He is co-author, with Jim Tomlinson, of a study of Labour's industrial policy in the Attlee years entitled *Industrial Efficiency and State Initiative: Labour 1939–51* (Routledge, 1993).

Peter Catterall
Examiner's Report

Question

Did the two world wars alter substantially the place of women in British society?

Student's answer by 'Sadaf'

The subject of women and their emancipation is one of great controversy. The two world wars have been seen by many historians as an important turning point for women. They believe the experiences of war changed the attitudes of many men about women, and about themselves, thus leading to the emancipation of women. Other historians contradict this and call it merely a myth of the times.

The two world wars required the mobilisation of British society as never before. Female employment rose during the First World War in total by 1,345,000, the only sector where it fell being one of the few areas of the labour market women traditionally dominated, domestic serivce. Many women's lives were undoubtedly changed for the duration of the wars. The question is whether these changes proved enduring once the troops returned from the front. Sadaf is, therefore, right to raise the issue of whether the underlying assumptions about male and female roles also changed as a result of the disruption of traditional social patterns by addressing the question of attitudes. It is, however, rather dangerous to couple this with the idea of emancipation. The question is asking whether the wars altered substantially women's place in society, not whether it emancipated them, a different question altogether. Sadaf has erroneously assumed that it amounts to the same thing. This neatly illustrates one of the pitfalls of historical writing. Language has to be used as precisely as possible, not only to avoid the mistake into which Sadaf has stumbled, but because words may mean different things at different points in time.

Sadaf is, however, quite right about the extensive debate between historians on this issue. It is to the various positions in this debate that she next turns.

Gail Braybon claims that there was a great belief by society during the years 1914–18 that a great change was occurring. Press and propagandists played a large part in promoting this idea. Much attention was paid by them to women workers. The newspapers, magazines and books were full of praise for their contribution to the war effort and how this was leading to a change in their position within society. However, many articles were merely propaganda. Exaggerated stories were written to attract more workers, focusing on young pretty girls at work. Details such as the long hard hours, the low pay and the boring nature of the jobs were conveniently left out.

Journalists reported how women were now taking over jobs which had previously been exclusively reserved for men, but even they expressed the temporary nature of the change.

When July 1919 came around this proved to be the case. The theory of a new role became a myth and all the work put in during the war by women was almost forgotten. Men's attitudes towards women's work remained unchanged. They feared that women would be kept on at their expense, and that they would be forced to accept lower wages. There was much encouragement by the Government for women to resign and return to their homes once the war ended and their employment was no longer required.

Arthur Marwick presents a more positive view of the effects of the First World War upon the status of women. Marwick believes that the war did mark a turning point. Women successfully carried out work which they had previously been believed incapable of. The introduction of universal military conscription in 1916 is seen as leading to a transformation in women's employment. He argues that the growth of large-scale industry and bureaucracy would eventually have brought about changes, but the wartime shortage of labour compounded these developments.

Marwick concludes that the effects of the war on women varied according to their class. Before the First World War upper and middle class women had been dependent on their husbands or fathers. They came to take jobs in business, medicine and the military. Earning their own money gave them economic independence. Marwick argues that their work gave them a new 'self-consciousness and sense of status'. For working class women he argues that the war allowed them to escape dressmaking and domestic service for low grade industrial jobs. Even though these still offered limited horizons they still paid better wages.

This provides a succinct summary of the debate concerning the effect of the First World War upon women. Sadaf clearly sees the main issue as being how far the war changed women's position in the labour market. This was indeed one of the most conspicuous effects of the war. A Central Committee for Women's Employment was set up almost immediately after the outbreak of hostilities, on 20 August 1914. This was more as a relief measure, to counter the widespread unemployment that many expected the war to bring to men and women alike. By January 1915, however, far from there being a surplus of labour, there was an acute labour shortage. The Government began to urge women to register for war service in industry and, later in the year, the new Ministry of Munitions began to urge the dilution of women into industry. This was naturally resented by male trade unions, already doing their part for the war effort and anxious to preserve as far as possible wage levels that were being eroded by wartime inflation. Women posed a great threat to these wage levels. Not only did they, as unskilled workers, threaten to undermine the differentials for skilled work the unions had been careful to maintain. They were paid less anyway. Indeed, employers in the past had not been adverse to turning to female labour as a way fo bringing down their labour costs.

This was not simply a matter of women's work being considered less valuable than men because of the strength differential. Lower pay rates for women attained across all categories of work, including sectors such as shop work where strength differentials were of little importance. This was true even of the Co-operative movement, which was a major employer of women before 1914. Some radicals in the Women's Co-operative Guild were suggesting equal wages by 1900. In 1907–8 the Co-operative Wholesale Society instead set minimum wages of 24s per week for men and 17s for women. This differential partly reflected the fact that most women had broken careers, ending work on marriage, though throughout the nineteenth century large numbers of women never married and remained in the labour market. More importantly, men's wages contained a 'social wage' element. Men's pay was larger because they, unlike single women, had families to support. This continued to be generally accepted, by women as well as men, throughout the inter-war years. In 1939 equal pay was still effectively confined to women working on the buses and trams.

In these circumstances the condition the unions attached to accepting, for the sake of the war effort, dilution through women workers was the return to the status quo ante *after the war. The irruption of women into the factories may have contributed to wartime improvements in canteen and washing facilities. It was men who reaped the post-war benefits. Most women readily accepted this, although some were clearly dissatisfied when their employment horizons were abruptly curtailed with the outbreak of peace. This had social implications as well. Domestic service, the main form of female working class employement was far more restrictive, and less well-paid, than the munitions factories.*

Sadaf, although mentioning the class-specific aspects of women's wartime employment, focuses on working class women. Opportunities for women of other classes were, however, opening out. The Sex Disqualification Removal Act 1919 made it unlawful to bar women from public office or civil and judicial posts. The first woman barrister qualified two years later. Nor has

Sadaf tried to contrast women's work during and after the war with the situation before 1914. She has told us nothing about this, but it is important to explore it fully if she is to put the effect of the war into perspective.

The early nineteenth century saw the exlusion of women from dangerous workplaces (such as underground in coal mines). In the later nineteenth century they benefited from the growth of clerical work, although some sectors which were later large employers of women, such as banking, were less welcoming than others. The Bank of England nevertheless took on its first female employees in 1894. Women also made some progress in the professions and, by 1900, there were some 200 women doctors. The total female labour force in 1914 was 5,966,000, about 31.5 per cent of the female population over ten. Even at the height of the Second World War this proportion never exceeded fifty per cent. Meanwhile, during the First World War, the previous resistance of some employers to female employment was permanently broken.

Changes in the workplace are, however, not the whole story. Sadaf's concentration on this aspect is surprising. The question, after all, refers to women's place in society. The focus is therefore much wider than Sadaf has chosen to make it. A whole series of other issues could have been addressed. Did, for instance, the war change women's position in the home? The assumption, even of Labour women's organisations in the inter-war period, was that women's interests remained strongly focused upon domestic concerns. Labour-saving devices were, in the inter-war years, to begin to reduce housewifely drudgery. The balance of duties of the sexes in the home, however, changed hardly at all.

However, in other ways the relationship between the sexes was changing. The last flourish of the sexual double-standards which had produced the Contagious Diseases Acts in the nineteenth century was Regulation 40D. This was introduced under the Defence of the Realm Act of 1914 to combat the wartime spread of venereal diseases. Under it any woman seen talking to a soldier could be arrested and summarily given a choice between being examined for VD or six months in gaol. This was clearly discriminatory since the responsibility for sexual purity and the penalties for sexual indiscretion were placed entirely on women. Strong opposition, however, rapidly rendered it a dead letter. Instead there was a stress upon encouraging responsible attitudes to sex and marriage amongst both men and women. This was one of the themes of Marie Stopes' Married Love, *published in the last year of the war. The implication was that women should have more control of sexual relations, a process taken a stage further when Stopes opened her first birth control clinic for married women three years later.*

This legislation was passed in a changed parliamentary context. The 1918 Representation of the People Act allowed women over 30 who were either householders or the wives of local government electors to vote in parliamentary elections for the first time. In the same year the Parliament

(Qualification for Women) Act allowed women aged 21 and over to stand for Parliament. These are further examples of wartime change that Sadaf should have mentioned, though whether they are directly attributable to the war itself is another question.

Maybe neither of these views are adequate. The war did definitely expand employment opportunities for women in professional fields, clerical work and the retail trade. However, attitudes clearly changed little; once the war was over women were removed from 'men's jobs'. These were jobs they had been said to be perfectly competent for during the war. Afterwards they were suddenly once again inadequate. The jobs they did have they were encouraged to resign on marriage. Their work was never considered skilled and women were never allowed to join unions.

After the war the Government encouraged women to return to being housewives and domestic servants. The Central Committee on Women's Training and Employment ran three courses, all concentrating on domesticity.

It is true that a marriage bar persisted throughout the inter-war period. Even the BBC introduced this in 1932 on the grounds that married women were taking jobs from single women who had no other means of support. Two million women would never find husbands after the First World War. In an era of high unemployment the marriage bar was widely applied, and accepted.

What is not true is the idea that women could not join unions. Although serious efforts to unionise some trades with high concentrations of women did not occur until the end of the nineteenth century, some groups of female workers were already organised before then.

What of the Second World War? Marwick again argues that this greatly advanced women's emancipation, a view shared by contemporary writers such as Margaret Goldsmith and Gertrude Williams. Harold L. Smith has, however, taken issue with Marwick's interpretation. He has shown that women's involvement in the labour market continued to grow. Even in the depression year of 1931 75.7 per cent of women aged 14–24 were in employment. Whilst some upper and middle class women may have been drawn into employment for the first time work, for the majority, was not a new experience, and not likely to change their attitudes.

Nor, in his view, were women that willing to work. Government persuasion was needed. In October 1941 a survey showed that of 1,000 women available for works 32 per cent were unwilling to do so. Nor were women any more enthusiastic to continue in employment once the war was over. Only 39 per cent of new women workers wanted to continue after the war.

The Second World War did bring more married women into the workforce. However, there is some evidence this was already starting to happen in the 1930s. Without the war this trend would probably have continued but more slowly. By 1950 private employers were removing marriage bars, but this development did not reflect the war but a post-war labour shortage.

War work was considered by most women to be frustrating, unpleasant, monotonous and repetitive. Women were also made to feel unwelcome by male workers. In addition, married women forced to work faced difficulties coping with daily household chores, children and work.

The Government only mobilised women as a last resort. It emphasised the temporary nature of the jobs held by women and after the war encouraged women to return to their homes. Nurseries set up to help working mothers were rapidly reduced in number at the end of the conflict.

Certain groups of women workers were being encouraged to stay in the labour market in the late 1940s; in the cotton industry for instance as part of the post-war export drive. What Sadaf says is, however, broadly true. Some changes were investigated during the war. Equal pay was, however, rejected for most categories of civil service work by the Royal Commission on the subject in 1946. The situation only began to change in 1951 when a movement for equal pay in the public services began in earnest. After resistance from the Government on grounds of cost they won a limited victory in 1955. The Equal Pay Act followed in 1970, but it was not until this was amended in 1984 that equal pay for work of equal value was at last conceded.

Thus, in answer to whether the two world wars substantially altered the place of women in British society I would argue no. Having weighed up both sides of the argument the view that there was little change holds more weight.

One of the strengths of Sadfaf's essays is that she has remembered to test her argument throughout, by putting both sides of the case. However, she does not draw these threads together in this weak conclusion. The conclusion should convincingly sum up the argument. Instead, Sadaf merely gives her opinion. This is unlikely to impress examiners. It is not sufficient for Sadaf to give a simple yes or no answer. There needs to be signs of thinking out the implications of her answer. If the two wars did not change women's lives substantially (a proposition which is defensible on her chosen ground of the workplace, but has not really been tested here for other areas), then why not? What were the barriers to change and why did the changes that did take place prove short-lived? To have addressed these points would have strengthened her conclusion enormously.

Peter Catterall is Executive Director of the Institute of Contemporary British History and visiting Lecturer in History at Queen Mary and Westfield College, London.

Index